Welcome To Your Life

Simple Insights For Your Inspiration and Empowerment

By
Ronny K. Prasad
Certified Life Coach and Mindset Trainer

Foreword by Warren A. Henningsen
Author of the international bestseller *If I Can You Can*

Copyright 2011 – Ronny K. Prasad

All rights reserved. No part of this book may be used or reproduced in any manner whatsoever without written permission from the publisher, except in the case of brief quotations embodied in critical articles and reviews. This material has been written and published solely for educational purposes. The author and the publisher shall have neither liability nor responsibility to any person or entity with respect to any loss, damage or injury caused or alleged to be caused directly or indirectly by the information contained in the book.

The stories and events described herein are provided from memory. They are intended to be enjoyed and to teach rather than to be an exact factual history.

First Edition
10 9 8 7 6 5 4 3 2

Cover Design by Cathi Stevenson
www.bookcoverexpress.com

Interior Design by Keith Leon & Rudy Milanovich

Book Edited by Heather Marsh at Classic Editing
www.ClassicEditing.com

Book ISBN: 0-9753668-6-6

Babypie Publishing
Los Angeles, CA

Reviews about WELCOME TO YOUR LIFE

"Are you looking for holistic happiness? Read this book! Ron has created a pathway for you to be inspired, empowered, grateful and motivated to transform your life for the better." – **Loral Langemeier, CEO/Founder of Live Out Loud, international speaker, money expert and best-selling author of the** *Millionaire Maker 3* **book series and** *Put More Cash In Your Pocket.*

"A great blend of insights, encouragement and empowerment from Ron!"
– **Dr. Marshall Goldsmith, million-selling author of** *MOJO* **and** *What Got You Here Won't Get You There.*

"Personal Growth simplified – that is what Welcome to Your Life is all about. If you are looking for personal growth, Ron will give just what you need!" – **Peggy McColl, New York Times Best Selling Author of** *Your Destiny Switch*

"A simple self-help book in which Ron cuts to the chase, and provides powerful insights into personal growth. Highly recommended."
– **Ari Galper, Founder,** *Unlock The Game®* **and** *The Home of Trust and Authenticity In The World of Selling*™

"A young author, sharing his insights to connect you with your authentic self. Know who you are, be who you are, love who you are. Welcome to Your Life!" – **Dr. Kevin J. Fleming, Ph.D , speaker, author of** *Half Truth High* **and President/CEO of Grey Matters International, Inc.**

"A creative blend of inspiration, empowerment, gratitude and awareness!"
– **Gerry Robert, best-selling author of** *The Millionaire Mindset*

"Deep insights from an authentic transformational leader. Welcome to Your Life!" – **Maura Leon, Vibrational Visionary, Director, Inner Light Coaching, co-author of** *The 7 Steps to Successful Relationships*

"Welcome to Your Life is more than just a self help book. It is a step by step guide to empower, inspire and transform you!" – **Bill Bartmann, National Entrepreneur of the Year**

"Ron inspires me. And through this book, like me, you'll treasure the day you discovered just how great he is with his ability to tell it as it is and to connect at a very deep level. You'll find yourself saying 'Oh yes, that makes so much sense!' And you'll be feeling that in every page."
 – **Paul Dunn, Chairman, Buy1GIVE1 [B1G1] and author of** *The Firm of the Future*

"Welcome to Your Life is more than just a book, it is a tool kit for designing your life!" – **Dan Caro, author of** *The Gift of Fire: How I Made Adversity Work For Me*

"There are two kinds of people in this life: Those who walk into a room and say, 'Well, here I am.' And those who walk in and say, 'Ahh, there you are.' Let us each strive to be an 'Ahh, there you are' person.'" This quote, by Leil Lowndes, exemplifies what I come to know and respect about Ron Prasad. He is an 'Ahh, there you are' person' and in his book, 'Welcome to Your Life,' he shares his knowledge and experience as a very caring nurturer and coach of people." – **Keith Ready, founder, A Gift of Inspiration**

"Ron's passion for positive changes in people's lives really stands out in this book. Welcome to Your Life!" – **Anton Uhl, Executive Producer, Emma Ranch Studios**

"The practices in Welcome to Your Life will bring more empowerment, inspiration and awareness into your life." – **MJ Ryan, author of** *AdaptAbility: How to Survive Change You Didn't Ask For*

"I have been working in the personal development arena for over thirty years, and have read many books along the way. All of them have a personal theme of what the book will do, and Ron is no exception. What I like about this book is its simple approach to get a foundation on how to start, and how to continue the development of individual potential!"
 – **John Kanary, author of the international bestseller,** *Breaking Through Limitations*

This book is dedicated to my beautiful parents who unconditionally gave me so much in life. Thank you for anything and everything!

Warren Henningsen and Keith Ready, my mentors in personal development, you have my utmost gratitude.

Kimiko Miyazawa and Linda McWaters, you got me started on the intriguing path of personal development.

Siba Abdelki, thank you for always believing I could complete this book.

Keith Leon, you made this book possible, brother. Your guidance in every step of publishing this book is something I will always remember! My eternal gratitude to you and Maura!

Heather Marsh, you are a wonder to this world my dear! I am looking forward to having you by my side in editing my next book. Sending you lots of love and gratitude!

Cathi Stevenson, you are a creative genius. Thank you for tapping into my mind and designing the perfect cover for this book!

Foreword by Warren Henningsen

A number of years ago, I met a young man with stars in his eyes. This man had such a strong desire in his heart to change the lives of others that in just meeting him my life was changed. I had no idea as to the extent of change that Ron was going to have on me for a number of years after this initial meeting.

Ron is a man of extreme integrity and moral fibre. He is someone that I am blessed to call my student, friend and, very recently, my business partner. I was overwhelmed with joy at the prospect of working with Ron as he developed his awareness through participating in the "Finding Zero" 10-week mentoring programming with me. As I suspected, throughout the course Ron's awareness *exploded!!* While all of my clients create massive change in both their personal and professional lives, on few occasions have I seen such phenomenal changes in an individual.

Ron is a man with an amazing amount of heart. He has such an incredible desire to see positive changes in others. In the following pages you will discover these qualities. You will come to know, not just the man, but you also gain an understanding of the soul this man possesses.

Before you continue reading, I recommend you get up, and find a pen and notebook. There are many thoughts and concepts that you will want to hold onto forever. Read, learn, write, absorb and apply.

Thank you, Ron. Thank you, for bringing this to us all. The world is a better place with you in it.

Warren A. Henningsen
Author of the international bestseller *If I Can You Can.*

Preface

Right now, you are holding in your hands the book I have poured my heart into. If you gain just one simple lesson from it and apply it to your life, I will be grateful for that.

The sole purpose of putting this book together was to make a positive difference in your life.

As an executive coach, I often mention to my corporate clients, *"Do not just make a dollar, make a difference."* That is the principle I have applied in this book. My goal is to encourage you to take control of your life and achieve the results you have been dreaming about.

The moment I discovered the purpose of my being, I realized I would compile a book and reach out to people on a mass scale. My goal was given more power when I began by writing a monthly newsletter and self-help articles which were embraced by thousands of people around the world. I strive to connect with my clients, whether I'm working one-on-one or speaking to an audience. I convey the same personal commitment to you as I do to them. I am connecting with you as if I knew you before you even picked up this book.

Life is truly a wonderful journey; full of experiences! I hope you embrace these experiences, and search for the sometimes hidden meaning behind every one, which I believe is part of a higher order!

I have shared with you my insights, personal lessons, ups and downs, advice from great mentors and teachers and, most importantly, I have shared with you my life. Yes, Welcome to My Life!

This book is a result of my collective experiences: the people I have met, circumstances I faced, countries in which I lived, challenges I have overcome, lessons I learned, times when I was touched by something higher than myself, clients who allowed me into their lives, audiences who heard me speak and were moved emotionally and intellectually to a higher place, readers of my articles, people who challenged and brought out the best in me, and the wisdom bestowed upon me by the greater universe.

I am sharing my story with you.

I began this journey by running away from whom I saw in the mirror; only to find myself on the path to becoming an inspired life coach, executive coach, personal development writer, and professional speaker who teaches people effective ways to find purpose and passion in their lives by living with passion myself. I am sharing these stories with you, because you are no different from whom I am.

My life began in an ordinary fashion. I felt I was just your average person, and continued that way, until I started focusing on the negatives in my life, with the intention to heal them. Until early adulthood, I had suffered a few major blows, and I kept holding on to these damaging experiences, not realizing how much they held me back. I was far from empowered and inspired. Then I embraced self acceptance and self love. With that, my self-awareness grew immensely! It was a liberation of my core inner being. It took a lot of inner work to get to where I am right now! The journey was worth every moment. Looking back, this book would've been ideal for me at that earlier stage in my life!

I found the purpose of my being. So can you.

You can live with passion and expect miracles every day.

I found it fitting to ask Warren Henningsen to write the foreword to this book, because one of the most profound lessons he taught me is "*If I Can You Can*", which is also the title of his international best seller.

So, I sincerely hope you gain insights here and apply them to find purpose and passion in your life!

Every word written in this book is for you, your goals, and your future.

It begins now!

Ronny K. Prasad

Table of Contents

Chapter 1:   Welcome to Yourself .... Page 15

Chapter 2:   Welcome to Awareness .... Page 33

Chapter 3:   Welcome to Acceptance .... Page 47

Chapter 4:   Welcome to Your Language .... Page 63

Chapter 5:   Welcome to Your Attitude .... Page 79

Chapter 6:   Welcome to Fear .... Page 97

Chapter 7:   Welcome to Discipline .... Page 109

Chapter 8:   Welcome to Gratitude .... Page 127

Chapter 9:   Welcome to Perspective .... Page 145

Chapter 10: Welcome to the Perfect Order .... Page 159

Chapter 11: Welcome to Higher Inspiration and
               Empowerment .... Page 181

Chapter 1

Welcome to Yourself

"You can achieve anything you want in life if you have the courage to dream it, the intelligence to make a realistic plan, and the will to see that plan through to the end."
Sidney A. Friedman

Life is all about choices. You have the liberty to choose. Choice is one of your birth rights. As humans, we have an abundance of choice. Just look around to notice every outcome is a result of choice. We make choices in our lives which have a bearing on results in all areas of our lives.

Right now, you chose to pick up this book and read it! You have taken a step in leading a purposeful life with passion, which approximately 97% of people shy away from. Why? It is their lack of awareness. Awareness is something I will encourage you toward in this book!

Most personal development experts will say you were meant to have a beautiful life. You then ask, how can life be beautiful when almost every day you're faced with adversities?

The answer is having tools at your disposal to rise above these adversities. Bob Proctor, whom I consider one of my teachers in personal development, said that, *"God never gives you a problem you can't handle."* Hence, even though you will encounter challenges, you can face them and reap the rewards. The reward depends on your attitude and determination to do whatever it takes to rise above or go beyond the challenges ahead of you. Whether you believe in God, a higher power, the universe, or life itself, Bob's quote can be applied to you.

The purpose of this chapter is to get you to examine and analyze 'you' by examining a broad range of topics, then the following chapters will focus on specific areas of your life. As you analyze yourself, you will gain very useful insights. I believe that this self examination will give you a better understanding of why you are here, who you are today, and why you have certain results so far in your life. Then, you will be in a much better position to make decisions and take steps towards inspiration and empowerment. I will suggest how to include these aspects of your life as you read through the following chapters.

Before we go any further, I would ask you to get a pen and notebook, so you can answer the questions that I will be giving you as we go along. Writing causes your memory to retain more. So, please keep your pen and notebook handy as you study this book. You can even write your favourite quotes as you move through the chapters!

You have already faced challenges in your life. The way you handled them defined your results. So, the core of this chapter is 'You'. As you read this chapter, please stay focused on the person closest to you: Yourself!

"Always be a first-rate version of yourself, instead of a second-rate version of somebody else."
Judy Garland

Please allow me to share some of myself with you, so you get an idea of where I am coming from, and some of the choices that I made.

As a young man, I graduated from university with a Bachelor's degree in financial planning and spent a number of years working in the financial services industry. As my awareness shifted, I chose to go from being a financial adviser to being a life coach, executive coach, and a professional speaker. Now in coaching and speaking I am doing what I love most: supporting people in having a purposeful life! It took years of studying myself to gain an understanding of who I wanted to become. Now, when people ask for guidance in finding purpose in their lives, I share with them what I went through myself.

I have figured out, through my work in personal development and sales, the most important topic for anyone is themselves. So, for the remainder of this chapter, please, let's concentrate on you.

Now, you and I will explore various aspects of yourself and your personal experiences. This is designed for you to start thinking about what motivates you and what holds you back, so you can move forward with greater joy and ease.

Most of your behaviour stems from what you have learned throughout your life. You learned from your parents, neighbourhood, schools, media, religion and associates. Learning is a never-ending process. The point to remember is that learning and applying your knowledge leads to conditioning.

You are unique as a result of what you have learned, applied, and conditioned yourself to believe; through your habits, childhood experiences, the desires of your parents, your religion, your likes and dislikes, and your unique perceptions.

Let us start by looking at your **habits**, which are things you have done so many times that they have become subconscious.

Your habits have a large bearing on what you have achieved and how you conduct yourself. Some habits have been replaced by your conscious effort, and others exist without conscious effort.

Think about a destination you regularly drive, walk, or cycle to. For example, let's say your goal is driving to the store for groceries. Your favourite market is near the gym where you like to work out. Without thinking, you might find yourself in the gym parking lot, because you automatically drove to the destination you're conditioned to seek so often.

> *"Where your pleasure is, there is your treasure; where your treasure is, there is your heart; where your heart is, there is your happiness."*
> **Saint Augustine**

Most of this book will focus on your life now and the life you want to create. I will also be sharing some of my insights and experiences with you. For a moment though, think back to your childhood and see how much it shaped your adulthood. *What was your childhood like? Would you relive your childhood if you could? Were you happy with your childhood? If you could change anything, what would you change? How would you change it?* I hear many stories of when people were physically, emotionally, and mentally conditioned to behave in certain ways as children, and then carried those traits into their adulthood, sometimes for the rest of their lives. Some of these traits serve people well, others have the exact opposite effect.

As a child, you learned certain important lessons from your environment. The **environment** that surrounds you had an impact on your character. As you got older, society began to shape you in other ways. What you saw, heard, and felt from your society had a bearing on your being. Most people think and act according to the environment that they are in. Certain iconic moments can stand apart from the rest, teaching you at times when you least expect it.

I recall, as an adult, during one very hot, post-summer March, I went to an Aboriginal Men's Camp designed to bring young Aboriginal Men together in strength and unity. The camp was next to the mighty Murray River, in South Eastern Australia. The locals there were excellent swimmers who were conditioned to swim in the river's currents. They jumped in, and started swimming with ease! I, on the other hand, had never swum in a river with such currents as the Murray River. I was accustomed to swimming in the sea. The currents of the river were beyond my experience! Whenever I went to the beach, I would jump into the water, and swim with ease. In the river, that was not the case. I found it very challenging to swim in the river.

I have shared this illustration with you to define how different environments can shape our expectations and experiences. Now, can you imagine if you were at the camp with me, and you had never swam in a river or sea, because you only had access to swimming pools, or never learned how to swim at all, or perhaps you are a talented swimmer? Your experiences and expectations of being in the water would have been very different from mine!

Other experiences in your environment will shape your character and personal habits. The people with whom you mostly associate, your family, friends, colleagues, teachers, and neighbours, will determine your character and behaviour to some degree. When you look at your lifelong experiences, notice how some of your behaviour has been shaped by the people you consciously allowed or chose to be a part of your life! If you associate with great people, eventually, their greatness will rub off on you.

Exercise

How has your environment shaped you? Where do you live (city, countryside)? How many people are in your immediate family? In your extended family?

How have the people you know and associate with shaped you?

Your experiences can be responsible for elements of your character. However, this does not mean your past equals your future. Certainly not! If you have done something repeatedly in the past and it has not served you fruitfully, you may learn that this is not the way to go. You can look back and learn so much for the betterment of your character. You always have the option of looking back at past experiences and using them to create more positive experiences in the future. Broadly speaking, experience is invaluable.

If you have not, until now, taken a good hard look at yourself, and asked some probing, meaningful questions, you could be missing out on living 'your' life. You might realize one day that parts of your life are a result of other people's choices and preferences. You could have easily made certain people into authority figures in your life, and then acted upon what they wanted you to be.

This scenario is common in families. I have noticed that, in certain cultures, children are brought up to follow the desires of their parents. Their careers, spouses, religions, dietary choices, sense of dressing, and recreational activities might be decided by their parents. This is, by no means, only applicable to certain cultures. This can be a universal quality.

This is also a common scenario in the workplace where an employee lives his professional life based on the ideals of his senior, boss, or manager. Well, in your personal life, is there a boss? Yes, there is. That boss is YOU!

Your **religion** (if you follow one)**, or your set of spiritual beliefs** could have exposed you to certain ideals and beliefs that shape your behaviours. For example, most of the Middle Eastern nations are Islamic nations. What you believe, in a religious context, can influence your behaviours and, in particular, your faith (not only in God, also in mankind).

If you are not into organized religion, your beliefs about religion will still have a bearing on you. I have seen time and time again, that people will impose their beliefs on you, regarding religion. I am only pointing this out, so you become aware of it. What you believe is entirely up to you.

Exercise

How has your religion (if you believe in one) shaped you?

Not only has the culture in which you were raised and your experience with religion played a role in how your life has been shaped until now, **your likes and dislikes** have much to do with your character and behaviours.

What determines your likes and dislikes? One man's treasure is truly another man's trash. A lot of your likes and dislikes can stem from experience and personal preference. From what I have read, seen, and experienced, most people will do more to avoid the things they do not want, than do more to get the things they do want.

This is a **theory of avoidance** as a primary motivation. For example, if you work in a sales role, you have to make a certain number of new contacts a week to meet your sales targets. This means that you have to pick up the telephone and do cold calling. If you have a fear of cold calling, you would avoid making them at any expense. You would create 'other work' for yourself, which would keep you away from making cold calls! So, the reason you might do the remaining work on your desk is because you are avoiding this one activity.

Your likes and dislikes also stem from the meaning you give to them. Avoiding something could be your motivation to create other work for yourself in an area you enjoy. For example, if you like to exercise, you probably see exercise as meaning fitness, fun, and vitality and are likely to be in good physical shape. The opposite could be said if you don't like to exercise. In that case, you might associate exercise with physical strain, exerting energy, getting tired, being sweaty and your physique is very likely to not be so fit. So, do you see the difference here?

I enjoy maintaining a personal fitness routine, and you will notice how I encourage you in this way as you read through this book. If you find exercise to be beneficial in your life, going for a long run in the mornings, five or six times a week, could be your fitness goal. When you start this routine, perhaps you begin with distance running and associate it with fun and vitality.

Then a trainer advises you to 'mix it up'. He suggests that you do sprinting on certain days. When you first start sprinting, it is a lot of hard work. Your hamstrings and quadriceps might be sore for days, after your first sprinting session! So you initially associate sprinting with pain! Then, you might tell yourself that sprinting will help you to get faster, is a good test for your muscles, and a quick work out! After learning to appreciate the advantages of sprinting, you might start to disassociate sprinting with just pain and see how fun it is! You won't avoid it anymore, because it initially caused pain. You could incorporate it into your running regime, and really begin to enjoy it.

As you can see, the theory of avoidance as a primary motivation can have a strong effect on people. It will trigger your mind to avoid doing something, sometimes at any cost, even if what you are avoiding is good or helpful for you! This is not productive in most cases. People tend to avoid things that could be ultimately beneficial to them, because it's easier to focus on short-term pleasure and avoid all pain, rather than risk experiencing short-term pain for long-term gain. If you look at my example of the cold calls, can you imagine how many business contacts you would have made, had you kept on cold calling? If you continued to associate pain with exercise, can you imagine how much you would have avoided doing any form of exercise?

"Learn to balance your perceptions, and begin to live with gratitude."
Dr. John DeMartini

Let's move on to perceptions now. Your **perceptions** shape your character and behaviours by all accounts. How you see something will determine how you feel about it. Perception is reality. When I was 19 years old and working in the kitchen at a restaurant, we were told the guests dining at the restaurant were always right. If I cooked a meal the guest requested and he did not like it, we supported the adage that he was always right, even if I had done my best to cook the meal according to the guest's request. The perception of the guest was always right, and, on occasion, it directed his choice to send the meal back to me in the kitchen.

On a larger scale, your perception, along with other factors, determines what is right or wrong for you and therefore will direct the path you take in life. Obviously, perception differs widely between individuals. Perceptions impact your decisions which, in turn, determine your end results.

Some people see their end results as their reality. What is reality anyway? I believe that reality is what you perceive. If the price of petrol had risen by about 10 cents per litre in the space of a day, you might think to yourself that it is expensive to put petrol in your car, because the price has jumped to about $1.30 per litre. If you have some relatives come from out of town, and they tell you that the price of petrol in their city was $1.90 per litre, suddenly your perception might change! My reality was that petrol was expensive here in Melbourne. Then I realized that it was very cheap, once I heard what my relatives from New Zealand told me about the petrol prices there.

Now, let's look at other things that affect your behaviour and habits. Consider how these next influences have affected your life.

Seeking approval for your deeds and words will make you act and behave in certain ways. I have seen many individuals who based their lives on seeking approval from others. In the process they gave their power away, and missed out on living their own magnificence. Their actions were based on the desire to please others. Do you fit in this category? If so, ask yourself why are you doing this? Believe me when I say this, just ask and the answers will come!

Exercise

What daily actions do I feel need approval from someone else?

What values and beliefs do I have that came from someone else in my life?

How would it serve me if I acted from my values, without seeking approval from others?

Seeking approval from others can result in disappointment for some and joy for others. I would suggest that you make an empowered choice when it comes to seeking approval from others.

Joys and disappointments will have a big impact on how your life is shaped. Certain people and circumstances have brought you joy in the past.

Why did these bring you joy? You felt that these were aligned with your desires and preferences.

How joyful did you feel at the time? You would gladly relive these experiences which brought you joy. You would do these things again, because you got satisfaction and fulfillment out of these things.

On the other side, certain people and circumstances have brought you disappointments.

Why were you disappointed? You did not get a desired outcome.

How did you feel at the time? Quite clearly you did not feel very satisfied or fulfilled. You would likely avoid these people and circumstances, because you associated them with disappointment from your past experiences.

I have also noticed that often people work hard to achieve balance in their lives, yet few seem to have it. Their tendency is to focus too much on one side of the equation. For example, if you work long hours daily, and sometimes weekends, you can miss spending time with your spouse and kids. To maintain balance that supports your core values, you can ask yourself, *"What is more important to me right now – spending time with my family, or earning more money?"* To create a balance in this area, you can set boundaries on how much you will work, and how much time you will spend with your family and friends!

If the above paragraph resonates, you are looking for more '**balance**' in your life. At this point, I would like you to realize everything in life is balanced, although not always in support of your core values. I will go into greater depth about 'balance' later in this book, in Chapter 10. It is one of my favourite topics!

Then there are **unique experiences** in your life. These significant events go on to shape certain areas. I call these "one off" experiences. For example, let's say you experienced something very powerful, and it shape the way you dealt with an area in your life from that moment forward. Some people are touched by a single, kind act from a total stranger, and their faith in humanity takes a massive leap forward!

On the contrary, you might have experienced a "one off" in your life which made you doubtful or fearful. For example, some people refused to fly in airplanes after the terrorist attacks in America on September 11, 2001.

These events have a bearing on your life, to the extent you decide. Your perceptions shape and direct your reality.

I will go into so much depth later on the subject of self acceptance, in Chapter 3, that you will need a scuba diving licence to discover it all!

Now, please address the questions below.

Exercise

Has a "one off" event in your life dictated some of your characteristics?

Since then, what have the results been in your life?

Are you happy with the results since the "one off"?

Is the "one off" controlling your life for the better?

I hope you learned something new about yourself after addressing these questions.

Your **potential** can have a big impact on who you are, if you allow yourself to realize it. Your ability cannot be measured. Most individuals do not know what their true potential is. Sometimes, you let what is outside of you dictate what you think your potential is. If you studied a career in school that you really enjoyed and the careers co-ordinator at the university, whose opinion you trust, says you will never get a job in the discipline you were passionate about, how do you think you would feel?

At times like this, you can become very negative and take to heart what others are saying or thinking about you. As I mentioned earlier, remember this is an exterior perception of you, or what someone else might think is best for you. Others may believe their perception is right, although it may not be right for you or the unique gifts you bring to the world. No one besides you knows your true potential. The onus falls on you to realize your potential to the fullest. Finding your true center, so you can stay focused and true to yourself, is part of finding your true purpose in life, which we'll touch upon in Chapter 10.

Imagine if, when you were in grade school, you wanted to be a track athlete. When you went to the athletics trials, the athletics teacher looked at you, and said to his fellow teacher, *"No, she can't compete."* This teacher had never seen you compete as an athlete. All he saw was a skinny, young girl who did not 'look' like an athlete. At the time, it made you feel like you were not good enough! You thought that he was right, that you couldn't compete. This is an example of when we are conditioned based upon other people's perception of us!

Once you got into high school, however, you realized that you could be a runner. You loved the thought of competing as a track athlete, and you knew you had the potential to be one. You see, at this point, you knew that what the teacher said in grade school was not applicable to you, unless you chose to take it on board! So, the same 'you' went on to compete in the high school athletics state quarter-finals. As mentioned earlier, your potential is just that, "yours". Not for anyone else to decide, it is only "yours".

Exercise

When have I felt that my personal ability, choices or actions were not mine to decide?

How does it make you feel that your personal ability is yours to own and decide for yourself?

As touched upon earlier in this chapter, **patterns in your behaviour** such as seeking approval from others, using avoidance as your primary motivation, or following a particular ideal that originated outside of you, does tend to shape your actions and hence, your end results.

One way to observe your patterns is to analyze your actions in one similar event or circumstance from the past and look for a link in your patterns of behaviour now, such as at work, with friends or in a romantic relationship. Ask yourself:

What do I keep doing?

Are my repeated behaviours working for me?

If they're not working, how can I make them work for me?

Other important influences on your behaviour and growth are your **personal defense mechanisms**. *Do you have a built in defense mechanism which does not allow you to reach your goals in life?* This can be a very common scenario. I have seen this in many people, myself included. Every time, you do not achieve a desired result, it's common that your defense mechanisms will automatically activate and give you all the reasons and excuses for not being able to succeed in that endeavour. I would strongly defend myself for not succeeding. Things such as *"I did not have the right support; no one believed in me; I tried and that is good enough for me; I am too this or that."* None of these excuses were beneficial to me. I realized I could do without all of them. Excuses never deliver the results you are seeking.

> *"Each experience through which we pass operates ultimately for our good. This is a correct attitude to adopt and we must be able to see it in that light."*
> **Raymond Holliwell**

Now, that we have looked at defense mechanisms, let's move on to morals.

Your **morals** certainly give meaning to your character and behaviours. You will act according to your morality when faced with everyday situations. In many cases, your morals have been ingrained into you from an early age. Your perception will change how you view what is for you, and what is not for you.

Let us look at moral issues in people. What you tend to believe is morally correct for you, may not be so morally correct for someone else. Once people reach the age of reason, they tend to start making moral choices for themselves, which are generally based on their values and ideals.

As a small child you may have wanted to give money to people less fortunate than yourself, and asked your mum for a coin, so you could. Now, at the time you might have thought it was a very moral deed to give money to others. You may have loved giving money to people less fortunate. However, as an adult you might realize some people use this money for alcohol or cigarettes, and now you may think twice about giving money away. Particularly if you find it immoral to financially support the drinking and smoking habits of another person. Hence, your sense of morality has changed your behaviour in regards to people less fortunate than you are.

This point is emphasised in the best selling book, *The 7 Habits of Highly Effective People* by Stephen Covey, where he makes reference to your creation as either by design or by default. This is important to understand. What you are, and who you are, is either designed by conscious effort on your behalf or it is defaulted to what seems to be acceptable and the norm in your life. Now, ask yourself:

Was I designed into what/ who I am now or was I just defaulted into what/who I am now?"

Now, I will stress that you are not your events or circumstances! You are you! That's all there is to it. Detach yourself from any situation, so you can see it objectively and act with more clarity. You are not that situation. If you were my executive coaching client, I would emphasize this. See what a relief it is to hear this message, to detach yourself from your circumstances. See what a major impact it has on your life, if you have a tendency to look at situations and get emotionally caught up in them. When you can view a situation without any attachment to it, it can work wonders for you. You can be calmer and at ease.

Lastly, the type of **questions you continually ask yourself** will have a major bearing on your life. For example, if you have a tendency to ask yourself, *"Why do things never work out for me?"* your mind will look for answers, and give you proof that things never work out for you! By the same token, if you ask yourself empowering questions such as, *"How can I overcome the challenge I am facing now?"* your mind will give you answers that allow you to overcome the challenge, and achieve a desirable outcome!

To sum up this chapter, I request that you study the insights you gained about yourself while reading. I hope you have learned something new about yourself. You have examined and analyzed yourself, to gain useful insights that give you a better understanding of why you are yourself, and why you have gotten certain results so far in your life. This puts you in a much better position to make decisions and take steps towards inspiration and empowerment.

I will suggest how you can work on these aspects as you keep reading through this book.

Self Assessment

Whose life have I been living so far: mine or a life designed for me by someone else?

_____

_____

To what extent am I letting outside forces shape my life?

_____

_____

If I were the ideal "me", what would I like to see?

_____

_____

Now, let's welcome you to the next chapter, **Awareness.**

Chapter 2

Welcome to Awareness

> *"The mind fixed in the awareness of the One is like a rock, unaffected by doubt, stable, secure."*
> **Sai Baba**

What is **awareness**? By definition it is *'having perception or knowledge.'* Now, knowledge is the key here! Knowledge of who you are. For the purposes of this chapter, I will be referring to awareness in the context of self-awareness.

So, what exactly does it mean to be self-aware? Well, it means to know yourself better than anyone else could ever know you. Has anyone ever said to you, *"I know you too well,"* or *"I know you very well?"* When people say that to you, they are coming from their perception about you. Let us focus on your awareness about yourself.

Whether I am working with a personal or corporate client, or speaking in front of an audience, I always emphasize the importance of being self-aware. When I am doing one-on-one work with my clients, my first step is to get them in touch with themselves! That is self-awareness.

So, what exactly does self-awareness mean to you? It means knowing the true you! At this point you might say, *"I know the true me. If I don't know the true me, who else does?"* If you really think you know the true you, this chapter will be a good test, or refresher for you.

> *What is the true you anyway? The true you is the total sum of:*
> *What you know about yourself*
> *How you feel about yourself*
> *What you see yourself as*
> *What your values are*

I like to begin my one-on-one life coaching work with one question:

What is important to you?

Please put this book down right now, and get a pen and notebook. Ask yourself the above question, and spend the next 3 minutes thinking through and writing your answers. Number your answers or put them in dot points. Please spend exactly 3 minutes. Anything longer or shorter may be counterproductive.

What answers did you come up with? Were there any surprises?

Once you have done this exercise, I want you to take it even further. Next to each answer or number, put the word "*Why?*"

Now, carefully take your time to answer the question, "Why?" It amazes me when I pose this question to my clients. I have seen blank expressions, surprised looks, and happy faces, when this question is asked.

For example, if you wrote down 'love' and 'family' as being important to you, your answers may look like this:

Love. *Why?* I want to love, and be loved. Loving somebody connects me with them, and I feel close to them. Being loved by others makes me feel valued, and I appreciate that.

Family. *Why?* My family means the world to me. They give me so much support and love in my life. I love them dearly. I will always support and cherish my family.

> *"Let us not look back in anger, nor forward in fear, but around in awareness."*
> **James Thurber**

That simple exercise is very valuable in connecting people with self-awareness. It is the first step.

Now that you have done this exercise, ask yourself this question:

What are my top 5 values?

Look for any congruency in your top 5 values, and the answers you wrote above to "*What is important to you?*" I do this with all my clients, and it gives them, and me, a clear sense of their values!

My top five values are love, gratitude, compassion, contribution, and growth!

Self-awareness, in its most basic form, is important for your survival. To increase your understanding of the importance of being self-aware, imagine being lost in a dense forest in the middle of the night. It is dark, you are in a totally new environment, and know nothing about where you are. At this moment, you will have a heightened level of awareness around you, because your safety is at stake!

Likewise, your ability to live a purposeful life with passion is at stake if you stay away from raising your level of self-awareness. The only person who can allow you to live a purposeful life with passion is you! So, help yourself by raising your level of self-awareness.

My mentor and dear friend, Warren Henningsen, is, in my opinion, the foremost expert in self-awareness. What Warren has shared with me and thousands of people around the world is priceless. Below is an excerpt from Warren's bestselling book *If I Can You Can*.

> *Unfortunately most of the global population still look at the world as it presents itself, through their perceptions derived from the pre-programming of their ancestors who lived in poverty, sadness or at the very least who lived with limitation of some kind, and assumed that they must change to fit within it.*
>
> *Instead, let me assure you that the world will fit to you if you are able to alter your perception, your paradigms, and your programming. Nothing can happen on this physical plane without it first being imaged in the mind or on the thought plane. You can create the life of your dreams, but first you must know what that life would look like. You need to open your perception to a point where the greater understanding is the only way that you see things.*
>
> *Try this exercise for a moment. Find a tube, or roll up a piece of paper or a newspaper and go and stand in front of a mirror. Actually do this and you will find that your "world may go from being flat to being round." Close one eye and look through the tube with the open eye at your own face. Is what you see through*

the tube a clear representation of who you are?

Now take away the tube, open both eyes and see yourself in your entirety. By increasing your level of awareness you enable yourself to see the bigger picture and thus you find you are more able to make an informed decision on what is real or more complete. Now keep in mind that even your full appearance may not provide a clear understanding of who you are, only what you look like as a whole.

I suggest that you do this exercise now, and see what perspective you get into self-awareness. Many people see the world through the tube that Warren mentioned. How could they possibly see what is outside the tube, when they look inside themselves? Obviously, they will miss a lot of things, including their true magnificence.

By the same token, if you only have tunnel vision when you look inside yourself, how can you expect to see the bigger, or holistic, picture when you look outside yourself? Often, this is something many people barely grasp until it is brought to their attention by someone whom they care about or an unexpected event!

"Every human has four endowments: self-awareness, conscience, independent will and creative imagination. These give us the ultimate human freedom... the power to choose, to respond, to change."
Stephen Covey

There are times in your life when you would question other people's actions and say, *"Why would he do that?"* or *"How could he do that?"* I hear this all the time, because I am strongly involved in the animal rights movement. When there is a story in the newspaper about a person abusing his dog, most animal lovers would react emotionally and think to themselves, *"How could anyone do that?"*

Through years of study in the personal development field, I have discovered that people do things as a result of awareness, and a lack of awareness. Once they increase their levels of awareness, they can certainly do things differently as their consciousness expands and their imaginations give them the power to choose, respond, and change.

I had a lack of self-awareness, until I got involved in personal development. Warren Henningsen really expanded my understanding, by teaching me first-hand how I could act through awareness, instead of a lack thereof. I began to understand that for every problem there was a definite solution, and that a solution could be reached easily and quickly. When I was acting through a lack of awareness, I would just focus on the problem at hand. Once I started focusing on the solution, instead of the problem, things started to change for the better!

In my late teens, I had a severe acne problem. It became so severe, that dermatologists prescribed oral and topical medication in the hopes that it would go away. I avoided looking in the mirror at all costs, and I cursed myself for being me! That is all I knew I could do.

I was absorbed in self-pity, questioned my life, questioned God, and hated whom I saw in the mirror. It was all I knew. I acted from a place of awareness, and a lack of awareness.

My awareness was that I should see a doctor in the hope to find a cure. My lack of awareness manifested in how I did not do more research about what caused the acne to be so severe, so I could address the cause, not the effect! I could have then looked into natural ways of overcoming the problem.

So, I took this path. After using pharmaceutical medications for weeks on end, my acne problem was solved. I was elated.

A few years later, a new, unrelated health issue arose. My digestive system had an unusual reaction to something I consumed and I developed little white spots on the side of my tongue. Unlike the acne situation, this time I knew I was in control of what I could do, and how I could respond. My awareness had shifted, and I was in a better place to handle this challenge. I was aware enough to look around for options! I researched the causes of my ailment.

Instead of just taking pharmaceutical medication, I decided to explore more natural remedies. I had been curious about natural remedies for most of my adult life, yet, I never explored natural medicine in more detail. So, I took the counsel of a natural medicine specialist, consumed the recommended herbs, and did healing energy meditations daily until my digestive system was back to its perfect working order.

Why did I do things differently this time? Simply put, my awareness had shifted.

Another example of how my self-awareness shifted and shaped my circumstance regards my weight. For most of my life, I 'thought' I had a weight problem. I was very skinny and underweight by all accounts. My lack of awareness told me only one thing – I am too skinny. Then through my increased awareness, I realized that being slim (at a healthy body weight), has so many advantages! I am a much better runner than I would've been if I were bigger in body size! I am agile, quick, and very active, due to my slim physique! I often catch myself saying, *"The once 'under-weight' body has made me a good runner!"*

> *"The first step toward change is awareness.*
> *The second step is acceptance."*
> **Nathaniel Branden**

Self-awareness is the first step, and it is ongoing. Let me elaborate on that. When you begin to raise your level of self-awareness, you will start noticing more things about yourself. My suggestion to you is to keep at it. Constantly raise your self-awareness. Let it be so, from now until your last days on Earth. Awareness is all about being in the present moment. When you wake up tomorrow morning, let that be your present. Right now, this is your present moment. Let self-awareness be part of your present moment at all times.

Make self-awareness a conscious choice. Choose to raise your self-awareness at all times, or even better, at times when you feel challenged by people or circumstances.

Regardless of what people or circumstances seem to do to you, only *you* can control your perception about them. This is important to remember; your level of self-awareness is determined by your choices! Carry this concept with you for the rest of your life, because it is worthy! To the masses of this population, this concept may seem very extraordinary. Why? They are not accustomed to questioning their knowledge of themselves.

Ask yourself a simple question right now:

Does my current level of self-awareness serve me well?

Be aware enough to be 'aware'. What I mean by this statement is simple. **Let your self-awareness create more self-awareness.** As you know now, self-awareness is an ongoing process. The more you create, the more will be created!!

Expanding your self-awareness will greatly benefit you. It will also be very beneficial to the people around you. Please share this concept with your family, friends, and associates. Ask them the questions I asked you at the beginning of this chapter: *What is important to you? What are your top five values?* See what their responses are. In your mind now, pick one person to share this with. Write his or her name in your notebook, and write down these two questions, with room for the response. Allow this friend to increase his level of self-awareness, so that he can take this amazing journey with you, too

> *"The world is not a problem;*
> *the problem is your unawareness."*
> **Shree Rajneesh**

Another benefit of raising your level of self-awareness is that it gives you greater options. When you have more options, you are in a better position to make more informed decisions. Have you ever said, *"I have no choice"* or *"I had no choice"?* Once your level of self-awareness starts to increase, those statements will be a thing of the past and your quality of life will increase.

When you have more options, you have more freedom. More self-awareness frees you up from feeling constricted or held back. You are more mobile; you can move in your desired direction.

If I were not fully aware of my capabilities to transform people's lives for the better, I wouldn't have the courage, ability, or foresight to write this book. My raised level of self-awareness gave me the vision that I could write it, and the courage to take the steps get it done.

Raising your level of self-awareness will also raise your self-worth. The better you know yourself, the better you will increase your self-worth. I do this exercise with my clients who are challenged by their self-worth. I get them to connect with their true selves, then I ask them to list all the things they like about their true selves. It is amazing how their self-worth increases!

I once gave a speech on 'Knowing Yourself' to a mixed group of old and young, white collar and blue collar workers. The people listening to the speech told me they were moved by it, and would apply the insights I shared regarding self-awareness. Everyone likes to help others in some capacity. Once you get to know yourself really well, you can get to know others better. Once you know other people, you are in a better position to support them.

I wrote the article below on self-awareness, and sent it to the subscribers of my newsletter.

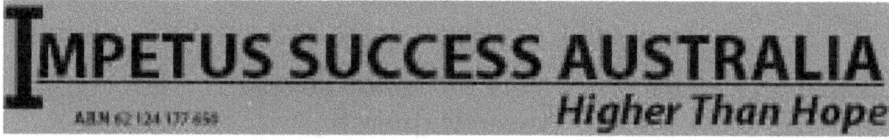

Greetings, and welcome to IDEAL INSIGHTS, a newsletter designed for people who are looking to make a positive difference in their lives.

Who are you?

I am often amazed by the responses that people give me when I propose the above mentioned question to them. When I ask people to tell me who they are, most of the time they tell me their name. That is a good start. Having said that, there is more to you than just your name. There is more to you than just what you do or what you have. There is more to you than what you may think.

That is why I talk about self-awareness to the people that I work with. In 2008, the importance of self-awareness was brought to my attention by my dear friend, Mr. Warren Henningsen. Warren is a self-awareness expert, and since that day, I have been paying particular attention to self-awareness in my own life, and in the lives of the people that I work with.

Self-awareness is about getting to know yourself better. You may now be wondering, how do I increase my level of self-awareness?

I would suggest a two-step process.

Step one, ask questions of yourself. What I mean by that is this, at this very moment, just ask yourself a simple question such as "What is important to me?" Or, if you wish to take it further, you may ask "What are my top five values?"

Once you ask yourself that question, answer them immediately. Write it down on a piece of paper or on a computer.

Step two, observe. Observe yourself and see if your thoughts, feelings, and actions are congruent to the answers that 'you' have written down. Observe yourself in different planes of existence.

Ask yourself questions such as, "Are my actions congruent to what is important to me, or to my top five values?"

For example, if one of your values was integrity (in the answers that you wrote), and you just found yourself having 'small chatter' behind someone's back, ask yourself this, "Am I being congruent to my value called integrity by having 'small chatter' behind this person's back?"

Questions such as these will give you clarity on who you are, and raise your level of self-awareness.

Self-awareness is all about getting to know yourself better: how do I function; what are my thought patterns like; what are my emotions like; what do I expect from myself; and what do I see myself as?

Come up with a hypothetical situation, and ask yourself, "What will I do in this situation?" The answer to this question will clarify your level of self-awareness by telling you more about how you function. Play around with this concept, and come up with different hypothetical situations, in which you ask yourself the same question again.

Once you get to know yourself better, only then will you be in a position to know other people better.

Raising our level of self-awareness serves us in the following way. The more self-aware you are:

The better questions you ask
The better decisions you make
The better actions you take
The better results you achieve

Self-awareness is all about knowing the person that is closest to you (that is you).

Self-awareness is all about knowing the person that you talk to the most (that is you).

Self-awareness is all about knowing the person that affects you the most (that is you).

So, after reading this newsletter, please ask yourself the following questions:

What is my level of self-awareness now?
Why is it important that I raise my level of self-awareness?
How will it serve me better, if I raised my level of self-awareness?

"To find yourself, you must look within, not with'out'."
Warren Henningsen

Yours in Higher Inspiration,
Ron Prasad

| Impetus Success Australia | www.impetussucess.com.au |

I received emails from people all over the world telling me that they found this article to be very insightful indeed. An executive director wrote to me, telling me that this was the first time he was introduced to such a concept. Now, this man was much older than I am, and it really humbled me to receive such feedback from him.

> *"I think self-awareness is probably the most important thing towards being a champion."*
> **Billie Jean King**

As I mentioned in my newsletter, raising your level of self-awareness will lead you to better questions, decisions, actions, and results. That is what self-awareness is all about. You may think that being self-aware is being selfish, because so much focus goes on your 'self'. How can you focus on the outside without having focused on the inside? If I could use an analogy, how can you keep feeding others without ever feeding yourself? Eventually, you will starve yourself to exhaustion or even death.

Although self-awareness has the word 'self' in it, self-awareness is more than just being about you. Self-awareness makes you look at both sides of every situation. It contains the understanding that you're being self-nurturing.

Self-awareness connects you with something greater. Something that you may not have known existed within you.

> *"What is necessary to change a person is to change his awareness of himself."*
> **Abraham Maslow**

Self-awareness is your birthright. No one can stop you from raising your level of self-awareness. The only person who is holding you back from being self-aware is you.

Be aware of who you are, not what others think you are!

The sixteenth century French Philosopher, René Descartes, said, "I think, therefore I am." Some people translated this to, "I know, therefore I am."

Please know that awareness and knowledge are two different sources. Knowledge comes from learning. Awareness comes from developing yourself mentally. Knowledge can be learned. Awareness cannot be learned, it can only be developed.

So, to conclude this chapter, seek to know who you are! Knowing yourself is an ongoing process. So, if you ever feel that you need to do more work on knowing yourself, you can use this chapter as a reference for later.

Self Assessment

In the first chapter's Self Assessment, we focused on your 'self' mode, and you asked yourself questions to reflect on "How have I been conditioned?" In this Self Assessment, you are now in 'you' mode and you can focus on "How has my self-awareness increased?"

How well do I know myself now, compared to before I read this chapter?

_____

_____

What have I learned about myself after reading this chapter?

_____

_____

How will I keep raising my level of self-awareness? What can I do daily, weekly, and monthly, or at any regular interval, to raise my level of self-awareness?

_____

_____

Now, let's welcome you to the next chapter, **Acceptance**.

Chapter 3

Welcome to Acceptance

"Accept and celebrate the fact that what you are today is a direct result of everything that's happened to you. It's pointless to wish things were different. Remember, if you change one thing, you change everything."
Michael Josephson

Acceptance is the act of agreeing to something. In the context of this chapter, I will refer to acceptance as accepting yourself – the way you are, and your circumstances the way they are. This puts you in a better position to make the changes you desire, from a starting point called acceptance.

More than that, I would ask you to accept your true magnificence. Every one of us has a true magnificence. Whether you have realized it by now, or are still on that journey, I am here to help you connect with your true magnificence.

Acceptance will truly shape your life for the better.

When I was 6 years old, I lost sight in my right eye, during a school yard accident. It took me years to accept myself. When I embraced my true being, despite my visual impairment, the beauty of living with acceptance revealed itself!

I have shared the magic of acceptance with my clients, audiences, family, friends, and with total strangers. This really opens up people's minds. This chapter is a perfect follow up to the previous chapter, because once you have come to know yourself, you are in the ideal position to accept yourself.

Know yourself, and then be you!

The legendary Bob Proctor, from whom I have learned so much, summed it up perfectly when he said:

"If I have to be free, I have to be me."

Then Bob goes on to say, "Not the 'me' that anyone else wants me to be. The 'me' that I want to be." That is a very good point to remember. I see many people who want to be someone they are not. They base their actions upon replicating others. Have you ever heard someone say, "I want to be like this person?" I have heard that statement time and time again. I was one of the people who used to say it. You look at certain people, put them on a pedestal, and idolize them. This stops you from being yourself. The 'you' that you are intended to be. You also minimize yourself in the process!

> *"Accept who you are, and then improve yourself."*
> **Graeme Alford**

What a brilliant piece of advice from Graeme Alford, author of the best seller *Never Give Up!* When you totally accept yourself, you are giving yourself the best starting point, in creating changes in your life that will lead you towards your goals. It is as simple as that!

When I told Graeme I would include his quote in my book, his message to me was to let people operate from a point of acceptance first, improvement second! I found that to be amazing.

> *"The only person that you are not in competition with is yourself."*
> **Dr. John DeMartini**

It is important to understand you will never be anyone else. You are uniquely you! Accept it, and live from that premise. It will do you wonders. Have you ever imagined what actors would do if they were asked to play themselves in a role? They would play that role better than anyone else on the face of this planet. Why? They are the only 'them'. You are the only 'you' on earth.

I simply love Dr. John DeMartini's quote. How appropriate is this quote for anyone looking outside of themselves for acceptance?

Well, if you are not in competition with yourself, then all you have to do is very simple – Be Yourself! That is the best gift you can give to yourself.

When you look outside of yourself for acceptance, you give away your control to others. When you give away your control, you give away your personal power. What happens next? You become disempowered, because you have given your powers away. That is why you should always look inside of yourself for acceptance.

In my newsletter titled *Who Are You?*, Warren said:

"To find yourself, you must look within, not with'out'."

The same applies to self-acceptance. You must look within yourself, instead of looking "with'out." People often live on the acceptance and approval of others. I have seen this time and time again, with my clients, friends, and family. What purpose does that serve? It's possible you may not know you behave in this way, or perhaps you do. It will take some self-awareness to know this about yourself. If you think you might be one of these people, please ask yourself this question: "What purpose does it serve for me to live needing acceptance from others?"

Answering this will give you clarity about how you view acceptance. The only person's acceptance that you need is yours. It is plain and simple. Accept yourself, the way you are, and the outside world will reflect that.

When I was in my late teens and early twenties, so many of my friends were looking for acceptance from the outside world. At the time, I knew only a little about acceptance. What I knew, I learned from reading books, listening to speakers, and reading articles in magazines and newspapers. I knew that "everything happens for a reason", to "be thankful in every situation", and to "be thankful for who you are." I was aware of these statements at a superficial level, without knowing their true meaning. I would talk to my friends about their true magnificence, because I knew something important was there.

The time in my life when I first connected with my true magnificence and started embracing self-acceptance, happened when I was 20 years old and had chosen to drop out of university. The course required that, during the third year, I go into the industry and gain a full year's work experience. There were about 20 students in my course that year, and I was the only one who did not get an industry placement.

I felt sad, defeated, lost, unable to continue, and confused, so I decided to drop out of the university. I did go back on a part-time basis, a year later. At the time I made my decision to leave, however, I thought it was the end for me at university. All sorts of questions were going through my mind: Why am I the only one who missed out on the placement? Was it because I was not good enough? Was it because I was dark skinned? Was it because no employer wanted me? My thinking was very negative and all of these questions kept consuming me mentally.

Then I decided that enough was enough, and I would do something with my life. At the time, I was working part-time at a restaurant as a kitchen hand and my income was enough to get me by. I was living at home with mum and dad, and they were very supportive of me. During this time, I became really intrigued about spirituality and wanted to know more about something higher, so I could understand what was happening in my life.

Since I was a little kid, I had been very interested in different types of religions, particularly Hinduism, Christianity, Buddhism, Zen, Jainism, and Rastafarianism. I had studied these religions informally, and now was the time for me to learn about spirituality, not religion. I knew that religion could be generalized to larger groups of people; whereas spirituality was specific and applicable on a personal level. My spirituality is only mine! So, I started digging deep into the reservoirs of spiritual knowledge. At the time, I did not have an internet connection at home, so I would go to a local library and research spirituality on the computer and in books. I read books which gave a spiritual message, rather than imposing religious views.

> *"Acceptance of what has happened*
> *is the first step to overcoming*
> *the consequence of any misfortune."*
> **William James**

There is a Buddhist temple in the city of Melbourne, where I used to go when I was at university. I would go there to talk to the monks, read books, and explore more about spirituality.

There was also a Christian bookshop in Melbourne that I had been to before. I went there, picked up their books, and started reading. There was a very knowledgeable and enlightened man who managed the book shop called Doug Fisher. I asked him to open up to me and share his views on spirituality. My hunger for spiritual knowledge became even stronger, so I kept talking to Doug. Over the years, our conversations have continued, so that now I regard him as my spiritual father, and I still love spending time with him.

Although some people I talked to were from traditional religious backgrounds, I wanted to get their higher knowledge on spirituality, not just their technical understanding of historical events.

After I dropped out of university and began my spiritual awakening, I spoke to as many people as I could, to learn their insights about spirituality. It gradually became clear that my mission was to connect with spirituality, and I was determined to do it.

My goal was to fill my mind with spiritual knowledge. I would drive to a lake north of Melbourne called Sugar Loaf Reservoir. To me, that is the most peaceful place on the planet. I would take a book with me, and just read all day long. So much for a university dropout, refusing to read books again!

My self-awareness shifted and I became aware of my higher self. Before going to bed at night, I would meditate, and search for answers, while hoping to connect with my higher self! I began to understand it was a part of me, more than just my physical existence. I realized that my physical body was being guided by something higher. So, I did research and asked myself many questions, such as, "What governs this physical body of mine?" Then, through books and talking to people, I got my answers!

"You are a spiritual being, in a physical body."
Bob Proctor

After about seven months of doing this, it finally dawned on me! I finally realized, what I had been searching for was inside me all along! I had never seen anyone go through this transformation, so when it happened to me, I was filled with surprise and wonder. Just like the story *Acres of Diamonds*, as told by Russell Conwell, I realized that I am a spirit. To be spiritual, I have to connect with my spirit. It had nothing to do with religion. I felt very enlightened when this dawned on me.

There is a very wise Aboriginal elder named Uncle Reg, whom I met through doing Aboriginal empowerment work, about which I am very passionate. Here we equip young Aboriginal people with the right mindset to live a purposeful and passionate life. Uncle Reg gave me a piece of advice which reminded me of my quest for spirituality during my early twenties. He said, "To connect a person with their true self, you must connect them to their spirit."

So, once I discovered that I was the spirit, I came to terms with self-acceptance. In my meditations, I would embrace who I was, and how blessed I was to be me! That could sound egotistical, yet it wasn't. By embracing my true magnificence, I could be more empowered to do more spiritual work in the world.

I put forward a statement you can use to feel empowered: "I give myself permission to be me, regardless of what others think about me."

I started loving my true self. Despite my status as a university dropout and visual impairment, I realized that I was truly blessed and accepted myself for the way I was. God created me the way I was. So, who was I to fight it or reject it? Well, how could I reject it anyway?

Gone was my victim mentality. I used to think that I was a victim of this world when things did not go my way. I began to see how having a victim mentality robs people of taking any form of responsibility for their lives.

Until that point in my life, people kept telling me that I was a beautiful person, although I didn't believe it until my self-awareness expanded. In the past, I was always loving, caring, and supportive of my friends, yet somehow I couldn't apply it to myself. In fact, at high school, I was known as the mediator or peace-maker. Whenever there was a fight between two of my classmates, I was the first one there to resolve it. Back then, I had no idea about personal development, spirituality, or my true self. I was just doing what I am suggesting in this chapter: being myself.

Although people I cared about said these positive things about me, there was only one person on the planet who needed to believe it, and that was me! Until my spiritual awakening, I did not believe the positive things people said about me.

When I was 19 years old, one of the waitresses at the restaurant where I worked asked me a question I had never been asked before. She was a lovely, bubbly young lady named Kelly. She walked up to me, with a perplexed look on her face and asked, "Ron, why are you always so happy?" Without thinking, my response wa,s "Because, I like being happy." It was not my spiritual enlightenment that was speaking here. I barely knew what spirituality meant back then. It was my true self speaking to Kelly.

> *"There are two primary choices in life:*
> *to accept conditions as they exist,*
> *or accept the responsibility for changing them."*
> **Dr. Denis Waitley**

I shop regularly at a local green grocer to get my fruits and veggies. There is a lady at the counter there named Lucy, whom I love having a chat with. One morning, I went there around 7:00am, in the middle of winter in Melbourne. The sun had just risen, so it was still cold. As I started chatting with Lucy, she asked me a similar question to the one Kelly asked, thirteen years ago. Lucy asked, "How can you always be happy so early in the morning?" I laughed and replied, "It is the best way to start my day." She laughed with me as well.

So, as you have just read, I discovered self-acceptance at age 21. I thought that process was complete, until I met Warren Henningsen, when I was 28.

The lesson I learned about self-acceptance was simply that unless I fully accepted my circumstances as they were, they would not improve. Regardless of how hard I worked to improve my circumstances, they would not change if I couldn't accept myself as I was. As soon I gave myself permission to be me, my life started changing for the better.

What I told Kelly and Lucy came from a place of self-acceptance that simply existed. The happiness that they saw in me came from my true nature, even when my general awareness at the time I spoke to Kelly was negative. I came across as my true self, a very loving, kind, giving person. The only issue was these traits were directed towards the outside world and not inward, toward me! I lacked self-love. That all changed when I met Warren, and now you will find out how.

Warren gave me a simple exercise, which blew my mind when I did it. I will share this exercise with you, and want you to do it just as I did.

Exercise

For the next seven days, once a day look in the mirror for 30 seconds, without saying or thinking anything at all. Just focus into your eyes. This will connect you with yourself.

After the even days, keep doing this exercise, this time you have to say the following words:

Thank you

I love you

Do this for seven straight days. Be sure to keep your mind clear. Just focus on the image in the mirror, and repeat those five words. Say it with passion. Say it like you would say it to a loved one. Put energy and intensity into it.

When I did this exercise for the first time, the effect was magical. I was almost in tears when I started telling myself, "Thank you, I love you." It was such a soothing feeling. The word 'acceptance' was floating all around me when I started saying those five words to myself. I felt acceptance in every cell of my being. I was at total ease with myself, despite all the self-criticism I had perpetuated for most of my life.

That is what self-acceptance is all about; loving and thanking yourself, despite how you may have felt about yourself in the past. With self-acceptance, there is no past or future; there is only the present. Yes, self-acceptance is always and only about the present.

The first time that I told myself with intensity, "Thank you, I love you," I felt so redeemed. Although I had found acceptance when I was 21 years old, this was the icing on the cake. After finishing the series of exercises, I called Warren early one morning to tell him how I was feeling, and what I then saw myself as.

He was not surprised, because he had done this process with hundreds of people before me. He said that most people build up so much junk inside them, that self-acceptance does not have room to enter the person. He went on to say people need to clear their internal clutter before they truly feel the magic of self-acceptance, and that is exactly what I had experienced! I experienced the magic of self-acceptance, and I urge you to do exactly the same.

Just start with the first part. Look in the mirror for 30 seconds. This exercise can be done at any time during the day. I did mine first thing in the morning. Do it at your own time, instead of making it a chore.

Put this book down, and only continue reading after you have done this exercise. Go now!

"Growth begins when we start to accept our own weakness."
Jean Vanier

Ok, I hope you had a breakthrough when you said those five words. Now that you've done it once, I urge you to keep at it for seven days, so it becomes one of your best habits. I will keep doing this exercise for the rest of my life. Having self-acceptance in your life at all times is just like having a fine physique. You have to continually do exercises!

As I mentioned in the previous chapter, my awareness made me realize the benefits of having a slim physique. My acceptance made me love my slim physique. I love timing myself when I am running, and I set a goal to break that time before a set date! It is times like that, when I thank my body for being slim in structure, because it allows me to run faster, longer, and harder. Acceptance of my body has done wonders for my fitness!

I wrote the article below on awareness and acceptance in my newsletter:

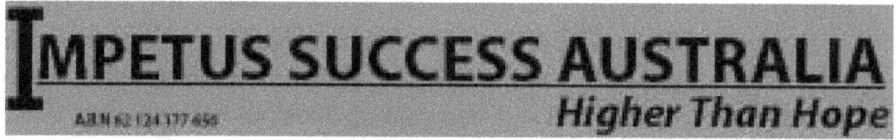

Greetings, and welcome to IDEAL INSIGHTS, a newsletter designed for people who are looking to make a positive difference in their lives.

Know, be and love.

In May, 2010, I wrote an article about self-awareness, which was later posted on www.myabsolutesuccess.com. I received much feedback from people who learned and applied the lessons in that article.

Knowing yourself is just the beginning. Acceptance and love are also required, when it comes to your holistic being.

Only self-discovery can lead you to your authentic self. This is something that I see in only a minority of the population. The masses of the population barely know their authentic selves, let alone accept and acknowledge their authentic selves.

In a recent speech on self-awareness, I suggested that people have to know themselves before they can know others. The same principle applies when it comes to helping other people. You have to help yourself, and then help others in the process. To be altruistic to the outside world, you must have altruism on the inside.

Once you know your authentic self, it serves you better to be your authentic self. Too often in life, I see people 'trying' to be someone that they are not. They put on a mask or persona, and in the process miss out on the opportunity to be their authentic selves.

Bob Proctor summed it up perfectly by saying, "If I have to be free, I have to be me." That is such a profound statement.

Regardless of what the outside world may like you to be, I believe that you will only live a life of fulfillment by being 'you.' Yes, I mean accepting the holistic 'you.'

If you accept someone else's ideals, you 'try' to live according to their authenticity, not your own. By doing so, you miss out on your own magnificence. Everyone has got their own magnificence, whether they acknowledge it or otherwise. It is your duty, to find and acknowledge your magnificence.

To truly unlock your magnificence, make a list of things that you like about yourself. Then, make another list of the things that you do not like about yourself. Make both lists as comprehensive as they can be. I would suggest that at this point, please completely ignore what other people like or dislike about you. At the end of the day, you are to live life for yourself!

Read this list aloud, and get emotionally involved. Be thankful for what is on both the lists. This is the key, be thankful for everything on both the lists! This exercise will let you tap into your magnificence. Then only will you come to accept the true 'you'.

After acceptance, comes love. Once you have accepted and acknowledged your magnificence, please realize how unique you are! There is not one single being on the face of this planet who is exactly the same as you! That in itself makes you unique. The more you focus on giving yourself love, the more love you will be drawing towards you, and the more love you will be putting out into the outside world.

Now, I will make this perfectly clear, that I am referring to self-nurturing love, not narcissistic love. Narcissistic love is not self love, it is selfish love!

Give yourself all the love that you feel you deserve. If other people in your life are worthy of your love, so are you!

When you become aware, accepting and loving of yourself, you begin to live life at a level, which only a small percentage of the population will ever experience. This type of living brings fulfillment and gratitude, which are two of the most powerful expressions of human existence.

Deep inside, every human wants to be known, acknowledged, and loved. You are the best person to start with. Give all of that to yourself!

After reading this newsletter, please ask yourself the following questions:

How much do I truly know about myself?
Am I being authentically 'me' all the time?
How can I give myself the same amount of love that I give to others?

Yours in Higher Inspiration,
Ron Prasad

Impetus Success Australia	www.impetussucess.com.au

"Know thyself, be thyself, love thyself."
The Delphi Oracle

At the end of my newsletter I mentioned that everyone would like to be known, acknowledged, and loved! Then, I suggested you do that for yourself first, before doing it for others. You are the ideal person to start this with! I used the quote from The Delphi Oracle to illustrate that you can only experience happiness with yourself if you know, be, and love yourself.

"There will be challenges to face
and changes to make in your life,
and it is up to you to accept them."
Anonymous

In concluding this chapter, I will leave you with the message that you are uniquely you. Everyone else is taken! You have got to be yourself. Nothing more, nothing less. Use the awareness that you gained in Chapter two, integrate it with what you can do to gain self-acceptance, and you will live a happier life! As simple as it sounds, it is necessary. I have done this with my clients, and I have done this with the person that used to be my biggest critic – me! You can do it, too.

Once you accept yourself, the outside world will begin to embrace you!

Self Assessment

How much self-acceptance do I have now?

_____

_____

What do I love about myself?

_____

_____

How will I keep raising my level of self-acceptance? What will I do to accept myself daily?

_____

_____

Now, let's welcome you to the next chapter, **Language**.

Chapter 4

Welcome to Your Language

"Your beliefs become your thoughts. Your thoughts become your words. Your words become your actions. Your actions become your habits. Your habits become your values. Your values become your destiny."
Mahatma Gandhi

Your language patterns (or your words), affect your life on a holistic level, and in many individual areas of your life.

To see how it works, do this experiment. The next time you are having a conversation with a stranger (or someone you have just met), consciously pay attention to their words. Focus on the patterns their words form. Just let them talk while you do the process of active listening. If you listen actively, you will learn so much about this person.

This is what I do with my clients, when I first meet them. I do very little talking, and just engage in active listening! What I gather from my new clients, just by focusing on their words, amazes me.

The same is true for you. Your words have a major bearing on the life you are living. When you become aware of the words you use to describe your world every day, you get a clearer picture of your unique reality. This works for everyone!

Now, when I refer to 'words', I am making reference to both your spoken words and your internalized words. What you say to others out loud are your spoken words. What you say to yourself are your internalized words.

To whom do you speak the most? Yourself! Of course, you speak to yourself the most. Many people have a voice inside that directs them more than they realize.

The power of self-talk is amazing, and more important than I could ever describe. Ask people you admire, in any area of their lives, about their self-talk. I bet that you will learn tons from them.

By the same token, go and talk to people who clearly need more empowerment and inspiration. You will find their self-talk is not supporting them. Hey, I was the number one candidate for that title. I had inspiring words for everyone except myself. I was so down that my self-talk was basically a dictionary for disempowering and uninspiring words!

Do you know people who are constantly experiencing ill health? If so, really listen to what they say to themselves the most. It is often something along the lines of, "Oh, my arm hurts! Oh, I am always sick and I'll never get better."

When I was constantly battling with life, my favourite sentence was, "Things never go according to my plans." This beamed disempowerment and had no sign of inspiration. Hence, I got exactly what I asked for.

Back then, I had zero idea about the perfect order, which is a full chapter in this book. Once you learn the perfect order, disempowering self-talk statements such as the above mentioned will be a thing of the past.

> *"I figured that if I said it enough, I would convince the world that I really was the greatest."*
> **Muhammad Ali**

Self-talk is programming the mind with feelings you attach to the words you use, when you speak to yourself.

Pay close attention to what you make your words mean, when you talk to yourself. Do not concentrate on their literal definitions, instead consider what you've caused them to mean. Pay particular attention to the feelings that arise. Words have a profound influence on the feelings they generate in you. Hence, we must choose carefully the words we use in self-talk. Empowering words will give empowering feelings. It is as simple as that. Please maximize the use of empowering words.

I was once conducting an event which I developed for business professionals, called the Corporate Mindset Training workshop. One of the attendees was a gentleman who said, "I can't" constantly. Obviously, his self-talk had ingrained these two words into his subconscious mind.

I asked him to join in a little exercise with me. He came to the front of the boardroom, where I was standing and delivering the session. I asked him to raise his right arm, by his side, at a 90 degree angle to his body. (Please refer to the figure below).

Then, I pressed down against his right arm, intending to take it back to its original position (to the side of his body), as in the diagram below.

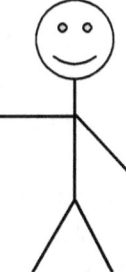

This is where the fun began. I asked him to keep repeating "I can't," with as much intensity as he could. He did just that. Guess what? I was easily able to push his arm down.

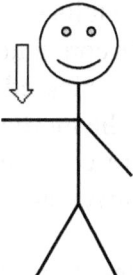

Then, I asked him to just relax. Again, I asked him to put his arm up, and this time I got him to keep repeating "I can", with as much

intensity as he could. Guess what happened this time? He could resist my arm without any more effort, even when I exerted more pressure on his arm. Why? It was the power of his words! Do this exercise on anyone, and see what eventuates! I was taught this simple and effective demonstration by Warren. It amazed me when I first did it!

The power of positive words always works. There is no exception at all. It is a universal law, as outlined by Gandhi's quote at the beginning of this chapter.

Some of your beliefs generate the words you use. Let us look at these beliefs briefly.

"Whatever things you ask for when you pray, believe that you will receive them and you will have them."
Mark 11:24

Beliefs can be defined as "acceptance of something as being true or actual." We all hold certain beliefs in the various areas of our lives. In some cases, our beliefs will be similar to those around us. In other cases, our beliefs will vary when compared to those around us.

Beliefs are formed in us as a result of what we are told, see, and experience. Beliefs can either be beneficial or detrimental to our welfare. Many people hold onto beliefs which were either fed to them by outside forces, or ingrained into them without much input from outside forces.

I have a belief that I am truly blessed. This is strongly ingrained in my subconscious mind. My mind tells me that I am truly blessed. I can say (through the use of words) with conviction that my mind automatically triggers the belief that I am truly blessed is true. My self-talk keeps repeating, "I am truly blessed". The more I say it, the more I see it! Just think back to the people who are constantly in ill health that I spoke about earlier. They say, "I am always sick," and they see evidence of it!

In my case, I believe it to see it, instead of seeing it to believe it.

If you are someone who finds it challenging to create empowering self-talk, please get your notebook and do this now.

Exercise

Ask yourself, "What would my self-talk be like, if my life was exactly the way I want it?"

Once you have answered that question, ask another question:

How can I apply this self-talk in my life, right now (without waiting for my life to be exactly the way I want it to be)?

Please write down the answers to these two questions, and focus on the message you get from these two answers.

"Whether you think you can or think you can't, you're right."
Henry Ford

There are two sides to your self-talk. Firstly, there is your higher self and then there is the little voice inside you. Your higher self is the part which is empowered and always works for your best. The little voice inside you is the biggest pessimist in your life. It always looks at, and focuses on, the worst case scenario. It does not work for your greatest and highest growth.

I use my higher self when making decisions in my life. My higher self guides me to my desired results. The little voice inside me speaks and lets me know what I should and should not be doing. I acknowledge the little voice inside me, though I never take its counsel. I am sure a lot of people have experienced something similar in their lives.

The little voice inside me used to dictate my life, until I put it back in its place!

Believing and wishing are two very different things. A classic example of this is when people confuse 'positive thinking' with 'wishful thinking.' Please be very careful when it comes to this. Wishful thinking can be very dangerous. The consequences of these two varied types of thinking are miles apart.

Simply wishing for something will not lead you to what you are wishing for. It does not encourage or motivate you in any way. It will not keep you focused on what you truly want. You have heard people saying, "I wish I had this or that". Simply wishing for something will not get you what you really want.

Positive thinking can be a great starting point to getting the results you desire. The point that I am driving to you is that the onus falls on you to create the results that you truly want in your life. You must take action. A goal is more than a wish. A goal is a wish backed up by a workable plan!

> *"The future belongs to those who believe in the beauty of their dreams."*
> **Eleanor Roosevelt**

You are presented with opportunities to empower your beliefs or create new empowering beliefs, every day. You can empower your beliefs by including powerful words. Using words such as success, strong, love, blessing, can, and power have a profound meaning on your beliefs. When you use such language in your spoken and internalized words, your beliefs automatically become empowering.

A statement that really got my belief working for me was the formula to success as given by Dr. Norman Vincent Peale, author of *The Power of Positive Thinking*. He said that we should use three words as a formula to success: "Believe and succeed." What a powerful message of hope, from one of the best teachers on the subject of positive thinking.

So, to sum up, your beliefs will have an impact on your words!

I strongly suggest that you read Chapter 13 of Warren's book, *If I Can You Can*. He gives very powerful insights into beliefs.

> *"It's the repetition of affirmations that leads to belief. And once that belief becomes a deep conviction, things begin to happen."*
> **Claude M. Bristol**

By this point, you have understood that your words are just that, yours! So, own your words, and decide on types of words you like to use in your vocabulary, both internal and external.

Here is a list of empowering words you can use on a regular basis:

Fantastic
Superb
Fabulous
Great
Brilliant
Amazing

You decide what you say to yourself, and to others. This brings me to using the power of your words to your advantage. I have been using affirmations since I stepped into the field of personal development, and it has paid great dividends. There are many ways to use powerful affirmations. I will give you insight on how to use words in your affirmations, to feel more empowered and inspired.

Affirmations are defined as the act to affirm or state positively that something is true. For the purpose of this book, I will refer to affirmations as telling our minds something positive that is happening.

> *"Language is the software of the mind."*
> **Les Brown**

Before I go any further, I will make a clear distinction between making effective affirmations, and just repeating words without any conviction or passion. Anyone can just repeat words without any effect. When you use affirmations, you must put intensity in your words, and feel their effect. If you affirm, "I am loved," then feel loved at the moment! By the same token, if you keep repeating, "I am loved, I am loved," and deep inside you feel that no one loves you, you are clearly giving yourself conflicting messages.

Repeating affirmations using positive and empowering words will give you more confidence, certainty, clarity, and capability. Now, let's break down these four very positive words:

Confidence – Repeating empowering affirmations will give you confidence in your words and also in yourself.
Certainty – Empowering affirmations will make you feel certain that you will get to your desired end result. And, this certainty

will boost your confidence.
Clarity *– By continually making concise, empowering statements about achieving your goals, what you want and will get becomes clear to you.*
Capability *– By using affirmations effectively, you will feel more capable of doing what you need to do to achieve your desired results.*

"You will be a failure, until you impress the subconscious with the conviction you are a success. This is done by making an affirmation which clicks."
Florence Scovel Shinn

The power of words is amazing. Just think back to a time when you said or heard someone say something that was not well received; for example, a disagreement with a friend. There are a few ways to go about expressing your concern. You could be very blunt and say something along the lines of, "You are wrong. That is not the case. Get your facts right before you talk." This could hit your friend like a ton of bricks and needless to say, he or she would feel the impact of your statement cast upon them.

On the contrary, if you were to remain considerate of the effect that your words had on your friend and avoid casting any judgment, you could certainly say something along the lines of, "I thought otherwise. According to what I know, it is quite different to what you are saying. Help me understand where you got this information?" Notice how the latter statement does not contain any judgment in it?

The bottom line from the above example is very simple. When you choose your words carefully, you remain in control of your verbal expressions and also become more aware of the effect your words have on others. While there is no guarantee how your choice of words will make anyone else feel, you can select words which are not likely to make someone feel hurt, belittled, or upset. Likewise, when you choose empowering and inspirational words in your affirmations, the effect it has on your thoughts, feelings, and, ultimately, actions is profound indeed.

"Belief consists in accepting the affirmations of the soul; unbelief, in denying them."
Ralph Waldo Emerson

Something I have discovered that works wonders for my clients and me, is to replace disempowering statements with empowering questions. So, if the person who is constantly in ill health makes a disempowering statement such as, "I am always sick, I will always be sick." She or he could turn this into an empowering question such as, "How can I heal myself? What can I do to become healthy again?"

Please, pause for a moment and ask yourself:

What is one disempowering statement that I tend to make?
How can I turn this around into an empowering question?

Effective affirmations will empower you. Affirmations will give you the belief that you can really achieve your goals. This belief is driven by the power of words. Once this belief takes over, it can grow stronger with more and more powerful affirmations. When you keep feeding the positive belief with more affirmations, your beliefs can enable you to create your reality as you want it.

Affirmations give you a sense of security. The more you effectively affirm, the better you will feel. I am not implying it will be easy for you to reach your goals once you start affirming consistently. All I am saying is that facing challenges will be easier with the use of empowering affirmations, because you will be in a better place or position to face these challenges.

I can say with certainty, and many personal development experts and teachers all around the globe will agree, that using empowering affirmations works. If you are doing this for the first time, please give it the opportunity to work and it will pay dividends.

Give empowering affirmations the time and attention they deserve. If you have not used empowering affirmations before, a good place to start is to say something to yourself that you like about yourself. Something that is simple and not too intense. An example of this would be, "I like my smile." Make a conscious effort to say this! It will lead to a more empowering feeling. Then you can create your own empowering affirmations. You will be grateful you did.

Take for example, a person who is low in confidence. Let's say that she lacks confidence when it comes to dealing with others, on both a personal and professional level. Then someone reminds her of her achievements in life so far. She makes a list of all these achievements, and reads them over and over again. She memorizes this list, and makes this her affirmation! She continually consciously affirms, "I am an achiever. I have achieved these things in my life." This affirmation will only empower her! Then, she can go on to create other empowering affirmations.

"Positive affirmations do work. An affirmation can help you replace a negative thought with a more helpful positive one."
Karl Perera

I thoroughly enjoy my affirmations. I have a big smile on my face when I say them, regardless of the time of day. Repeating affirmations should be an empowering and enjoyable exercise. Once you get to a certain stage, it will come without effort. My favourite time for doing my affirmations is when I go for a run in the mornings.

Affirmations are effective. I had heard a song once where the singer talks about being on stage, while the audience is applauding. I really loved the way the singer expressed himself. So, I kept repeating the lyrics of that particular song. I kept saying, "As I am on stage, the crowd is applauding," without even realizing it. I was doing this subconsciously. I just loved saying these few words from this song. Many times, I caught myself saying those few words. It was never my intention to be on stage for any purpose or to be applauded by the audience.

Then on a fine sunny, spring afternoon in Melbourne, I was presenting at a financial planning seminar. I had done very little public speaking at this time of my life. At the end of my presentation, when I thanked the attendees for their time, they all started clapping for me while I was still on the stage! The applause went on for a while. I felt humbled and really felt their appreciation. It was not until a few hours later that I paused and realized that what I had been saying to myself from the lyrics of this song had actually come true. I did not intentionally repeat this affirmation because I wanted to be applauded on stage that day. I just kept saying these words subconsciously and it turned into reality. It clicked and I was totally blown away by this experience.

That night, I called my friend, Linda McWaters, and told her about my unique experience. Linda was thrilled to hear my little story and reminded me that affirmations will work even though we do not take them on board on a conscious level. I came to the realization that what Linda was saying was true indeed, by what had happened to me earlier that day. It amazed me that the power of words can work, even if we do not intend them to do anything for us in any special way. This is true for everyone. Although, in my example, the subconscious application of words was so powerful in turning what I said into reality, it was never my intention to use these words as an affirmation.

This is one point that I wish to emphasize here. Affirmations can and do work, whether or not we realize it. Hence, we have to be careful what we affirm on a subconscious level. It is worthwhile to give ourselves a self-check every now and then to determine what we are affirming subconsciously.

"One comes to believe whatever one repeats to oneself sufficiently often, whether the statement be true or false. It comes to be dominating thought in one's mind."
Robert Collier

I will now give you some of my favourite affirmations, from some of the best self-development teachers in the world.

"I am now ready to receive, and there is so much to receive, the abundance never ceases." Dr. Susan Jeffers

"I have unlimited power at my disposal." Kerry Riley

"I am responsible for my life, for my feelings and every result I get." Bob Proctor

"God is with me. God is helping me." Dr. Norman Vincent Peale.

"I am blessed with life." Phil Evans

"I am a genius and I apply my wisdom." Dr. Paul C. Bragg

Another great affirmation that Bob Proctor teaches is, "I am so happy and grateful now that I am...." You can complete the words after "I am". For example, "I am so happy and grateful, now that I am able to run for half an hour without stopping!" or "I am so happy and grateful now that I am confident during public speaking!"

Use reasons in your affirmations. The effect of this is two-fold. First, it connects you with what you are affirming, and second, it confirms that you choose and deserve what you are affirming.

For example, "I achieve all my goals, because God is supporting me all the time."

Affirmations are designed to convince your mind that what you are saying is true. The key is to keep doing it on a continual basis. I can assure you affirmations will not work if you do them inconsistently, or if you do them only when faced with a challenge.

Be committed to your affirmations when faced with big challenges as well as when it's just an ordinary day. Never permit your affirmations to fade or weaken. Persist with your affirmations. To make them really work, choose a specific time of the day or evening, and do them consistently. Then, watch the power of affirmations work its magic in your life. Work on your affirmations, and they will work for you!

So, your words define you and your world. Pay particular attention to your words. Use them to your advantage.

Self Assessment

How will I pay particular attention to my words, now that I am aware that they're important?

_____

_____

How will my beliefs support me in using empowering and inspiring words?

_____

_____

What is one affirmation that I will create and use daily?

_____

_____

What is one dream or desire to which I am now ready to allow my words to lead me?

_____

_____

Now, let's welcome you to the next chapter, **Attitude**.

Chapter 5

Welcome to Your Attitude

"Our attitudes control our lives. Attitudes are a secret power working 24 hours a day for good or bad. It is of paramount importance that we know how to harness and control this great force."
Tom Blandi

Attitude is defined as a state of mind, behaviour, or conduct suggesting some thought, feeling, or action. Your attitude in any area of your life gives the world a clear message about how you feel and respond to that particular aspect of your life. Attitude is very important, indeed.

Please pause for a moment and ask yourself, "What is my attitude in particular areas of my life?" Pick one simple aspect of your life in which your attitude is apparent to yourself and the outside world.

There are also certain areas of your life where your attitude is obvious to you, and not to the outside world. You can explore these areas by using the same strategy below.

Now that you have observed a certain attitude in your life, please address the following questions:

How did you form this attitude?

What is this attitude doing for you?

Are you controlling this attitude, or is this attitude controlling you?

You are ultimately responsible for your attitude in all aspects of your life, which brings me to my next point. You must take responsibility for your own attitude. You have the power and ability to control your attitude in every aspect of your life. Your results will be boosted by a more empowering attitude. There are wins, lessons, and experiences.

Welcome To Your Life

"A happy person is not a person in a certain set of circumstances, but rather a person with a certain set of attitudes."
Hugh Downs

People sometimes allow an experience to create an attitude for them. Have you ever heard anyone say, "I can see you're in a bad mood?" In most cases, the "bad mood" has been created by an event or circumstance. For example, you miss a meeting due to heavy traffic. You feel stressed while you are driving in traffic, because you're stuck, aware that you are going to miss the meeting, and, yet, you can't control the circumstance. Upon missing the meeting, you get into a very bad mood. The fact that you missed the meeting did not create the bad mood for you. You allowed the circumstance to create the bad mood for you. Well, in that case, the event or circumstance is controlling you!

As I said at the end of Chapter 1, you are not your results. You are not your circumstances, either. Detach yourself from any situation. Only then, can you be in control of your attitude. It is so easy to allow a situation to dictate your thoughts and, therefore, your attitude. The moment you do that, you have lost control of your attitude.

You are always in control!

If your attitude is negative and causes you to have lessons and experiences that are painful, and you desire to change it, then you must learn and take the necessary steps to empower your attitude. The onus falls on you to recognize and acknowledge the impact that an attitude has on your outcomes in life.

The power of attitude has made a significant difference in the lives of my clients who had goals to lose weight or quit smoking.

"Your vision does not create an attitude.
Your attitude creates a vision."
Ronny K. Prasad

One of my clients wanted to create an empowering mindset to support him in losing weight fast. From my experience, I have seen that losing or gaining weight needs three key ingredients: diet, exercise, and mindset (which incorporates attitude). I had been troubled by my weight for most of my life, so I was sympathetic to the pain he felt. People always told me I was too skinny, and I often listened to them, which caused my internal self-talk to make me feel small.

When it came to putting on healthy weight, I knew what to do in terms of exercise, diet, and mindset. I share this with my clients who wish to get in better shape, whichever way they define their goals.

This particular client wanted to lose weight quickly, so I worked on his attitude to ensure that the most empowering attitude was within his control. He had to exercise early in the morning, stay off excess sugar and fats, and remind himself to stay focused on his very defined goals! If he created an attitude that getting to his desired body weight would include too much pain, discomfort, and inconvenience, I bet that he would have gone off track and kept the excess weight on.

I told him to keep focusing on his goal to lose the weight quickly, and to keep reminding himself that his new diet and exercise regime was a result of his goal! At the end of every session with him, I would ask, "What is your attitude about your ideal weight now?"

His usual response would be, "If it's to be, it's up to me!" He impressed me with his commitment, and I loved hearing about his progress in getting to his ideal weight! He was a very driven young man and I knew that, with a bit of support, he would achieve his goal. Whenever he felt he had to put forth an extra effort to achieve his goal, he would remind himself of his affirmation, "If it's to be, it's up to me!" That is how he maintained his momentum!

As you can see from the above example, goals in any area of your life will benefit from having an attitude which is complementary to your goal.

Attitude can have a profound effect on your perception of events. In another touching example, the whole world saw what the Black Saturday bush fires did to the state of Victoria, Australia on Saturday, February 7, 2009. Being a resident of the Northern Suburbs in Melbourne, I am close to some of the bush fire affected areas. In fact, I lived in the municipality of Whittlesea, where the bush fire victims from Kinglake (one of the hardest hit towns in Victoria) had been given shelter.

A week after the bush fires, I was in the town of Whittlesea to drop off pet food that my friends had kindly donated to the local veterinary clinic. My dog goes to this particular vet, where they had been caring for many of the burned, injured, and homeless animals.

Driving back from the veterinary clinic, I was deep in thought as I had seen such suffering. So many people had been affected by the bush fires. On a brighter note, the overwhelming show of support and generosity from the general public was inspiring.

I was listening to the radio, when a lady who had been affected by the bush fires called in. She was expressing her gratitude towards the generous offers of donations that had been flooding in since the disastrous fires had struck, a few days earlier. When asked by the radio program host how she was feeling, her response was very powerful. She replied, "Well, I have got two options, I can either be BITTER or I can be BETTER. I choose to be BETTER."

What an empowering statement this lady had made. She had lost every material possession; yet, she felt empowered and was looking at the bright side of life. I could only imagine what trauma she had initially gone through.

She probably knew people who had lost their lives, yet, she was expressing gratitude for the fact that she was still alive. She saw this as an opportunity, not an adversity. She went on to say that she would move back to her home and rebuild. Now, that is a true definition of courage!

What a wonderful lesson for everyone. I can say with certainty that her empowering attitude must have been beneficial and inspirational towards the people around her, whose predicament was the same as hers.

This lady stood firm and remained hopeful, because of her attitude. Right at this moment, as I write this chapter, the Australian state of Queensland is experiencing its worst flooding in history! 75% of the state is affected by the flood. As I watched the news, I saw a man who had lost everything, except the clothes he was wearing, make the following comment, "As long as my family are OK, I am happy! I am grateful for that. We will rebuild!" What an empowering attitude to have!

> *"Attitude is the foundation of all success."*
> **Bob Proctor**

An empowering attitude will do wonders for you. Do you remember my client whose goal was to lose a certain amount of weight by a certain date? He linked his attitude to what he was working towards. This gave him an empowering attitude. Can you imagine if he linked his attitude to the challenging steps he went through to lose this weight? His self-talk would be along the lines of, "Oh, another long, tiring, and sweaty bike ride early in the morning. Then a breakfast of plain, wholegrain cereal in low fat soy milk, with no sugar! How will I get through this?"

He knew better and, thankfully, he enjoyed the exercise regime and healthy meals. So, the key is to link your attitude toward your empowering goal!

You observed one of your own attitudes at the beginning of this chapter. Now, you can observe the attitudes of people around you.

Here's an exercise for the next few days.

Exercise

Pick two or three people that you are close to and clearly observe their attitude towards certain parts of their lives. What do you see in their attitudes? Are their attitudes driving them forward or pulling them back? This can be a great learning exercise as we tend to learn from people around us.

If the people you observe have attitudes which serve them meaningfully, chances are you can learn from them and put in place similar attitudes for your own benefit. By now, you know about awareness, so your awareness will encourage you to learn empowering attitudes from others.

Just start observing their attitudes in their daily life. You don't have to wait for a crisis to hit them, to see how they handle it. You will learn a lot from them, by just observing their attitudes each day. I know people who are always smiling and happy! It is their attitude that drives them to be like this!

Attitude observation is a learning process which teaches you what to adopt and what to avoid. I am suggesting you could learn from other people's attitudes, and then evaluate your own. After you observe other people's attitudes, please follow this simple three-step process:

Exercise

Compare other people's attitudes to your own.

Question their attitude, and yours.

Refine and empower your attitude.

I'm not suggesting that you to compete with other people's attitudes. Nor am I saying that you should just blindly take on someone else's attitude. It is helpful to look at other people's attitudes, to see if this helps you to refine and empower your attitude. What works for them, may not necessarily work for you, so pay particular attention to what you are comparing!

When you observe someone whose attitude is that every challenge in life is an opportunity to grow, you may wish to take on components of that attitude, and see how they fit into your life. Some of your friends and family might have very empowering attitudes, and it may be good to apply that into your life.

You can also find inspiration from notable figures in history. I've been inspired to design this book around motivational quotations I've collected. Every one of these people has a great story to tell. I would encourage you to read more about them, to gain inspiration and motivation in your own life.

Hearing the lady who called the radio station taught me a great lesson about having an empowering attitude when circumstances seem to go against what I expected. This lesson came in very handy for me with a particular client I encountered soon after.

> *"It is our attitude at the beginning of a difficult task, which more than anything else, will affect its successful outcome."*
> **William James**

When I met this new client, she had limited funds and asked me to be her life coach. She was having a crisis in many areas of her life, so I agreed to give her a 'gift session,' in which my goal was to get her started taking control of certain areas of her life.

Our first session took place over coffee at a cafe in my local area. This session lasted for two and a half hours. We had breakthroughs and she was in tears for most of the session. At the end of the 'gift session,' I decided to give her another 'gift session' a week later. I truly felt empathy for her, and wanted to support her in being empowered and inspired.

Three days after the second gift session, she called me at 10:00pm. It was Sunday, and I was having a family dinner that night. She called me three times between 10:00pm and 10:30pm, and I missed her calls. The very next day, she sent me an email telling me that I really let her down by not receiving her phone calls. She accused me of being unprofessional, made a few allegations, and threatened to contact her lawyer.

I was surprised at her sudden change in behaviour and emailed her back. I told her our life coaching sessions were to cease immediately, and requested that she refrain from further contact with me.

At that moment, all sorts of thoughts could have gone into my mind, such as "I helped her for free, and she was so disrespectful and unappreciative."

What I discovered was this person loved playing the blame game. She blamed me for things that were her responsibility. I firmly understood that not all people in a crisis would be so negative or blame those attempting to help them. I also realized that some people will behave in this way. So, I detached myself from the situation, and realized that she was just doing what she was good at and had learned to do, by blaming others.

In that instance, I remembered the powerful words of the lady who called the radio station after the bush fires. I told myself that I am BETTER, not bitter after this experience. Then, I made changes to protect myself, so I could continue serving my clients and the community.

I discovered several reasons why I was better, because of the experience:

From that moment onwards, I decided not to grant 'gift sessions'.

I added to my disclaimer notice that I am available for access to my clients during business hours only.

I accepted that there are people who will do what they can to put me down if they have the chance to. I have to protect myself from such people.

After the above realizations, I had so much gratitude for this person. To this day, I have nothing except gratitude for her!

This is a classic example of how other people's empowering attitudes can help us to empower our own attitudes. I listened to the lady who called the radio station, and decided to learn from hers!

> "Attitudes are the drivers of our lives.
> Who is driving your attitude?"
> **Ronny K. Prasad**

My dear friend Ari Galper, founder of what I believe to be the most powerful sales mindset training in the world, Unlock the Game, shared this story with us on his website www.unlockthegame.com, about his son Toby. Ari posted this article on 17 December, 2007. I am privileged to be able to share this article with you! So, thank you Ari.

Lessons from Toby

In the past few weeks, I've been reflecting on an important part of my life that has taught me some lessons I wanted to share with you.

This holiday season really began for me and my wife Michelle on December 14 — our son Toby's second birthday. We had a party for him with about 15 other little kids aged from about 2 to 5.

It was a great afternoon. Some of the kids played together, while others played on their own. And there in the middle of it all was Toby, riding his little red-and-yellow car around the room and climbing up his climbing steps, just like all the other kids — doing his own thing but obviously feeling connected to them.

Except that he is a bit different. You see, Toby was born with Down's Syndrome. Some children with Downs Syndrome have serious physical disabilities and developmental problems. We're fortunate because Toby is physically healthy except for some low muscle tone. And he learns and does things more slowly than other kids.

But what hit me during his party was how naturally he seemed to fit in. Although he's a little boy who's "different," on his birthday he was just one of the other kids, and they treated him like anyone else, just as Michelle and I do.

The party made me think about a lot of things — for example, how we all have expectations about how life is going to be, and what happens when things don't turn out the way we thought they would. When Toby was born and we discovered that he had Down's Syndrome, I suppose it was natural for us to feel overwhelmed at first.

But as I was watching him playing at his party, I realized how much I've learned since he came into our lives. Here are some of what I've started to call "Toby's Lessons" that may help your new year get on the right track:

* Live in the present moment

Although Toby is different, he's also just like every little kid before they start learning to spend most of their time in the past or the future the way we do as adults. At his party, he wasn't wondering when it would be over or what would happen next. He was just in the present moment with the other kids — riding around, eating his cake, enjoying watching them.

So one of the most important things I've learned is that when I'm with him, I have to let go of my other concerns and just be there. I really value being with him — seeing his delights, his upsets, how he sees things and interacts with them — and I've realized how much I miss if I'm not in the present moment too.

* Slow down and focus

Because Toby does things more slowly, I have to listen and pay close attention to him. If I start speeding on ahead, the connection between us gets lost. So he has taught me to focus and slow down. Remember the "good old days" before we all got used to the idea that we should be multitasking at every moment? Well, Toby can't multitask. He does one thing at a time, and more slowly than other kids, but he does everything with total focus. That's been such a valuable lesson for me.

* Don't let things get to you

Toby has also taught me to not let things get to me so much He seldom gets upset, he laughs at everything, and he basically loves everyone he meets. He somehow seems to intuitively respond to them as whole human beings because he's too young to do any judging.

* Stop judging — none of us is perfect, but we're all unique

Toby's openness and lack of judgment has made me think a lot about what we tend to think of as "normal" — how our expectations and preconceptions sometimes blind us to what's there in front of us. I know that sometimes other people may see that Toby looks "different" and perceive him as not being "capable," when in a lot of ways he just does things more slowly. But people who don't know him may judge him as "less than...," rather than someone with special, unique qualities.

This is ironic because aren't all of us vulnerable to being judged as "less than..." in some area? After all, as human beings we all have our "imperfections." We want other people to be open to learning who we are, just as I want to be open to learning who Toby is, and I hope that other people will be open to that too.

I guess the main point I want to make is, maybe it's time for us to let go of ways of thinking about how we view the world and other people that may be holding us back.

This is ironic because aren't all of us vulnerable to being judged as "less than..." in some area? After all, as human beings we all have our "imperfections." We want other people to be open to learning who we are, just as I want to be open to learning who Toby is, and I hope that other people will be open to that too.

At his birthday party, Toby was just like all the other kids, and also as unique as they all were, and as we all are. Maybe if we can learn from him how to be a little more in the moment, with more patience and openness, and to recognize that we're just like everyone else — and also uniquely ourselves — we'll find it easier to reconnect with the best parts of ourselves as human beings.

In that way, maybe Toby is the way we all ideally could be.

Peace and happiness,
Ari Galper

Ari Galper is the creator of Unlock The Game®, a new sales mindset that overturns the notion of selling as we know it today. His profound discovery of shifting one's mindset to a place of complete integrity, based on new words and phrases grounded in sincerity, has earned him distinction as the world's leading authority on how to build trust in the world of selling. His personal insights on how to build trust between buyers and sellers continue to break new ground in the sales industry. You can take a FREE TEST DRIVE of Unlock The Game by accessing Ari's free audio seminar "7 Sales Secrets Even The Sales Gurus Don't Know!" at www.UnlockTheGame.com

I sincerely hope that you enjoyed the valuable lessons that Ari has shared with you in this powerful article. There is so much to be learned from Toby, which adults sometime overlook!

Now you can take a moment to reflect on what Ari's article has done to your attitude.

Ask yourself the following questions:

What will I do to live in the present moment?
What will it take for me to slow down and focus?
How will I detach from situations, so things do not get to me?
What can I do to see the uniqueness in others?

Then continue reading the remainder of the book! Please feel free to contact Ari directly with your thoughts on his powerful article, ari@unlockthegame.com.

"Your attitude affects everything in your life and here's the best news – you control your attitude!"
Dave Boufford

One of the most powerful books that I have read on attitude is *The Winning Attitude* by John C. Maxwell. In this book, the author makes clear suggestions on how to develop a winning attitude. John C. Maxwell quotes that, "Often our attitude is the only difference between success and failure". I am a very strong believer in that statement.

Have you heard of people who did not give up against all adversities, and finally succeeded? And then there are those who gave up at the first encounter with adversities and, needless to say, did not succeed. The difference between these two individuals is their attitude. The successful person had a "never die, don't give up" attitude and this drove him to success eventually. Whereas the one who gave up had an attitude of "I am faced with a challenge that is too difficult. I will not be able to do this."

These two individuals could be equally talented, equally equipped with the necessary requirements and equally skilled. However, one of them had an empowering attitude and the other did not.

Mr. Maxwell further quotes, "Our attitude can turn problems into blessings". What a beautiful way to look at things when we are faced with problems. As sure as sunrise, I can say with confidence that we will encounter problems. There has never been a human being who never had to face a problem.

The lesson here is to see problems as blessings. Blessings which enable you to learn, develop, and evolve. Blessings which enable you to strengthen your character. There is an old proverb, "problems bring out the best in us". That could be said for everyone. It is then up to you to see it in that regard and make the most of the blessing the so-called problem presented to you.

Having an empowering attitude can be challenging at times. There will be times when you may feel knocked off track and your empowering attitude can be shaken. To maintain an empowering attitude, you must constantly look for ways to improve your attitude in all areas of life. I continuously remind myself that attitude growth is personal growth!

"Problems are gifts and blessings in disguise."
Kerry Riley

One common mistake people make is to avoid problems. Your attitude will not benefit in any way if you avoid problems. When you avoid problems, you are basically walking away from an opportunity to improve your attitude, grow, learn, expand, and engage with the world. When you do this, you are then letting your attitude serve you to the best of its abilities. There would be no opportunity for growth or improvement, if you were to walk away from your problems.

Please allow me to say something emphatically here. Sometimes, we are wise to avoid problems. For example, if you are walking home late at night, and you see a group of people acting suspiciously on a dimly lit road ahead of you, you would be smart to avoid them!

However, anyone with an empowering attitude knows they can't avoid problems all the time. They will see the problem as a great opportunity to strengthen their attitudes and work on the problems with the aid of their empowering attitudes.

Problems can be great teachers if your attitude allows you to thus perceive them.

I was once consulting with a client who wanted to request a justified pay raise at work. He felt very uncomfortable approaching the CEO of his organization to ask for a justified pay raise. He saw that as a problem.

I simply asked him, "Do you think it will be beneficial to you if you avoided this problem, or do you think you could find a solution?"

So, I asked him to write down all the reasons why he deserved a raise. In our next session, he showed me all the reasons why he wanted one, including the fact that he had managed to cut costs and increase productivity, invented new systems and procedures, and was conducting new training for the staff on a regular basis.

The question I then posed to him was this, "Now that you have completed this list, do you feel you deserve a raise?"

His face lit up, and he felt worthy of the pay raise. I asked him to give me a possible solution to his problem, which was to ask the CEO. He stated that he would show the CEO how well he had served the organization, and he felt he deserved it.

As it happened, the CEO was more than happy to reward his efforts!

The lesson here is that avoiding the problem was not beneficial at all. By focusing on a solution, instead of letting his fear about the problem stop him from taking action, he found his attitude helped guide him to better action steps.

He realized that what initially seemed like a problem, turned out to be a great opportunity. He was pleased at that realization! His attitude towards asking for a raise changed straight away!

"Every adversity, every failure, every heartache carries with it the seed on an equal or greater benefit."
Napoleon Hill

The people who find solutions are the ones who personally grow at a constant rate. Those who avoid problems, have little personal growth.

Everyone has the ability to choose, as mentioned in the first chapter. We can choose our attitude carefully and wisely, and then our attitude chooses the circumstances. Faith is greater than fear. Have faith in your attitude and let the faith overcome any fears you may have about reaching your desired outcome. I will talk about fear more extensively in the next chapter.

Your attitude is one of the greatest and most potent weapons at your disposal. You can have an empowering attitude. Just remember, it takes work and the work is greatly rewarded!

"People who have a positive attitude, are inspired, motivated and passionate about what they believe in, communicate better and more effectively."
Keith Ready

Self Assessment

What is my attitude towards various aspects of my life now? Please, be specific when answering this question. You can ask, "What is my attitude towards my career, my relationships, my health?"

_____

_____

How will I create a more empowering attitude?

_____

_____

Ideally, what would I like my attitude to be?

_____

_____

If I bumped into myself in twelve months, what would I like to see change about my attitude?

_____

_____

Now, let's welcome you to the next chapter, **Fear**.

Chapter 6

Welcome to Fear

"Fear is a natural reaction to the unknown. It is a guide that tells us to take precautions and to look before we leap. That is why, once we attain that which we were seeking, we are no longer in requirement of Fear and thus are no longer guided by it. By accepting Fear as a friend we no longer find ourselves focusing on eliminating it, which is a negative forceful act that draws more Fear to us. Thus, we enable ourselves to focus on the results we seek instead of the Fear that is stopping us."
Warren A. Henningsen

Fear is an emotion that is excited by threatening or impending pain, accompanied by a desire to escape it. People have fears of different sorts. It could be something as simple as a fear of tasting something bitter to as significant as the fear of heights. Either way, fear is a force strong enough to take over any area of your life and lead you away from your goals.

Please take a moment and ask yourself:

What do I fear the most? In other words, what is my single biggest fear?

Once you answer this question, please read your answers aloud. Do this twice.

Now, please answer the following questions:

How long has this fear been inside me?
Where does this fear stem from?

There are many books on fear in the market, and there are fear courses as well, designed to help you overcome them. What I have found is that overcoming the fear of something requires you to work on both your inner self and your outer world. How much work is required? That depends on what you are willing to put in to overcome the fear.

Welcome To Your Life

Ultimately, the elimination of fear can be done by only one person, YOU. You create your fears. You eliminate them.

I will go into detail on how to use fear to your advantage, and eliminate it in the process, later in the chapter.

Now, I would like to talk about a very common fear I have seen in people. That is the fear of success. Contrary to popular belief, it is not the fear of failure that holds people back. It's the fear of success. I have seen this over and over again. Initially, I thought that the fear of failure was holding me back from doing certain things. Once my level of awareness increased, I dug deep and realized that the fear of success was what I needed to eliminate.

On a conscious level, people may think they are fearful of failure. What I have found is that many are fearful of success on a subconscious level. Now, please bear in mind that your subconscious mind controls your results in life by allowing you to see only the outcomes it wants you to see.

Let's break this down. Take the example of when I began looking for a new employment opportunity. After having decided to advance my career, I decided to move on from the position I held at the time. I was looking for a better job, yet on a conscious level, I was fearful that I may not reach my goal. I had many disempowering, fearful thoughts and was certain I would fail. My negative internalized voice got louder and I would tell myself that I might not perform well at a job interview. When I saw a job vacancy in the paper or on the internet, I would tell myself that my credentials were not worthy enough to secure the role. Even though my goal was important, my fear held me back.

> *"In order to succeed, your desire for success should be greater than your fear of failure."*
> **Bill Cosby**

On a conscious level, I would get fearful before writing an application letter. The fear would be multiplied before the job interview! Fear would consume me to the extent that I started expecting I would not perform well during the job interview. It was a self-fulfilling prophecy.

When I did manage to secure a new job, my fear increased! Believe me when I say this, my fear of achieving my goal was greater than my fear of failing to reach it. Much of this fear came from the uncertainty that I was about to face! I was fearful of the unknown; of what was about to come. Even when I was successful in securing a new role to advance my career, I was fearful of what the future might hold in the new role!

Instead of being proud that I had secured a new job, I began to worry about the next problem that might happen. I couldn't enjoy being in the moment. As soon as I secured the new role, the fear of success gripped me again. It happened all the time.

My fear was broken down into:

The fear of change (new workplace, colleagues, travel routine, responsibility, systems, technology).
The fear of telling my existing employer that I was leaving them for another role, so I could advance my career.
The fear of losing my existing colleagues as friends.

Now, that I look back at those experiences, I realize I was more fearful of success than failure. The fear of the unknown gripped me. I had no fear of failure if I did not secure a new role with better opportunities for career advancement, because I would still have my existing job! I feared when I became successful in securing a new role and the many unknowns I would have to face!

I have noticed this with many people. Subconsciously, they ask themselves fearfully, "What if I do succeed?" They start thinking forward with fear. I was one of these people.

Exercise

Choose any area of your life, and take yourself through the process. Focus on one goal which you desire to achieve. I am referring to a goal, not a mere wish! Remember from Chapter 4 that a goal is a wish backed up by a workable plan!

Now, write this goal down.

Next, ask yourself:

***Am I fearful of failing to achieve this goal?
If so, why?***

List the fears that come up.

Then, imagine you have achieved your best possible desired outcome.

Ask yourself:

What will I fear, once I achieve this goal?

List the fears that come up now.

By doing this exercise, you are analyzing the fears that are involved in achieving a goal and you're giving yourself the gift of solving a new problem before it has a chance to happen. What a kind act you're undertaking for yourself. Great job!

We will go through the process of overcoming more fears as this chapter progresses further.

The key to success is to acknowledge the fears that come up. By avoiding fears, you could be avoiding achieving your goals.

Fear is to be embraced, not fought. You may be thinking, "How can I embrace fear?" Well, my question to you is. "How can you fight fear?"

Once you embrace fear, you are prepared for whatever is causing you to be fearful. As I mentioned in Chapter 2, acceptance is a great starting point. So, accept the fear that you have.

> *"Let your courage respond to needs that you see,
> not to the fear you may feel."*
> **Anonymous**

Sometimes, people get so caught up in their fears that they totally overlook the opportunities for growth and achievement in front of them.

I learned about the "dark room analogy" during my life coaching training at The Coaching Institute in Melbourne. One of the trainers mentioned this in a teleconference I attended in 2007.

You are placed in a totally dark room and are given a flashlight. When you switch it on, and the light focuses on a wall in the room, you see written on that wall are words like "uncertainty, worry, stress, failure." These words are very disempowering.
Then you turn around and focus the flashlight on another wall in the room, and you see written on the wall words like "power, love, motivation, growth, inspiration, hope, faith, success." These words are very empowering, so you feel good when you read the words on this wall.
Then, all of a sudden somebody turns the lights on and now the once dark room has been transformed into a room full of light. There is no need for your flashlight as the whole room illuminated by the light. Now, you see the whole room. You see both the walls. Both the walls exist and the words on the walls are around you.
The flashlight is your focus and the room is your existence. The "Dark Room" analogy is showing you that both walls are around you all the time. What you choose to focus on is your decision, and it, in turn, decides how you feel about yourself, your results and your role in this world.

Some people choose to focus their flashlight on the wall that makes them feel fearful! By focusing it constantly on this wall, they totally miss the other wall which makes them feel empowered!

Now, let's do a process which will encourage you to embrace fear, and then overcome that fear.

"Whatever you resist, persists."
Eckhart Tolle

The first step is to take fear, embrace it, and accept it. Just remember, if you resist fear, it will keep coming back. Resistance of fear will only hold you back.

Once you embrace the fear, you are in a better position to use the fear to help you move forward.

Then, ask:

What is this fear telling me?

Make a list of all the things the fear is revealing to you. Let's go through a practical example of how to do this in the next few paragraphs.

After completing that list, make another list of action steps:

What can I do about what the fear is telling me?

"Courage is the mastery of fear, not the absence of fear."
Mark Twain

Once you have written down action steps, you are in a much better position to overcome your fear.

When I first started my business, I feared making cold prospecting calls to generate new business contacts. Although I had made cold calls in the past as a Financial Planner, making them for my business was a very fearful experience. I would do anything to avoid making cold calls. I would 'create' other work to stay busy, so I would have an excuse not to make cold calls.

Then, Warren took me through the process of overcoming the fear of cold calling.

So, I asked myself, "What is this fear telling me?" I came up with answers such as:

I must:

Be prepared and present professionally.
Be confident.
Believe in my services.
Have absolute conviction that I can help people/businesses.
Take the 'sales pressure' off the person I am speaking to.

Then I asked, "What can I do about what the fear is telling me?" I came up with answers such as:

I must:

Prepare a list of questions that I will ask.
Prepare a list of responses to questions that I will be asked.
Have responses to objections that I may face.
Find out from the recipient of the call if I can add value to them/ their business.
Strongly believe that, 'If my potential clients have a problem, I have the solution.'
Be relaxed!

After making these two lists, I carefully analyzed what was creating the fear of cold calling, where it stemmed from, and what I could do to overcome it. I also joined Ari Galper's program and he put the icing on the cake by making cold calling an easy task!

Warren Henningsen said that fear is like a jacket. Put it on, use it to give you the information that you need, and then take the jacket off when it is no longer required.

My fear of cold calling gradually disappeared, because I used the fear to prepare me! Most of the population stays in fear and avoids what it fears! Imagine how many areas of your life you could improve by making this one change in your attitude.

To overcome any fear, you will have to take risks. This is true in all areas of your life: relationships, career, family, finances, and health. Having said that, the rewards can be tremendously beneficial. I am referring to calculated risks, as opposed to gambling!

Risk and reward are interrelated. A person who does not take any risks at all, the so-called Mr. or Ms. 'Play it Safe', may miss out on many opportunities that lie in front of him or her. I believe that if we use our intellect and intuition while taking risks, we are likely to receive the rewards that come with taking risks. When I commenced my own coaching practice, it was a big risk for me. Many people told me not to open a small business, because the chances of a small business failing are very high! I knew that if I did not take this risk, I would not be following my calling, and would miss out on living my life to the fullest!

As a financial adviser, I used tell my clients:

Risk equals Returns.

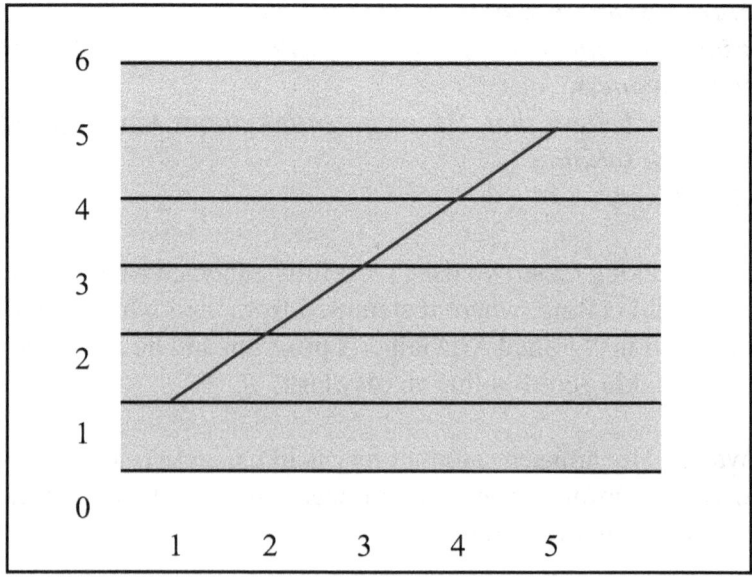

Now, this statement was once directed at my clients who wished to invest in an asset class with exposure to the stock market. However, you can expand this statement and apply it to other areas of your life. Without taking risks, there isn't much chance of getting any "returns" on your actions.

I took a risk by leaving the workforce when I started my own business. Many fears surfaced at the thought of doing so. I knew I would have to take calculated risks! It paid off, big time!

Through my experiences, I realized fear stands for:

F – faster
E – easier
A – available
R – resources

That is my definition of fear, because that is all fear is. It gives you resources to deal with what you are fearful of faster and easier.

"Approach everything in life with trust, not fear."
Drayton Boyleston

As I mentioned earlier in this chapter, the fear of success mostly stems from the fear of change. People are not afraid of change. They are afraid of being changed!

I once had a very intense session with a client of mine, who wanted to start building his business and leave his paid employment. He was a very dynamic, vibrant, and energetic person. He told me he knew exactly what he must do to build his business, yet something was holding him back.

I asked him a series of leading questions and, halfway through the session, he discovered, subconsciously, he feared being successful! Once he came to this realization, it came to his conscious mind that there were fears such as "I would lose my friends, I would have no time for my personal life, I may change as a person."

The thought of being successful in building his business triggered certain fears that prevented him from moving forward!

I worked with him to overcome these fears until he viewed his success in business without any fear at all and was actually excited to embrace the opportunities that once frightened him.

To conclude this chapter, please remember that fear is here to serve you. Use it to your advantage, and it will allow you to move forward!

Self Assessment

How will I embrace fear in one new area, instead of resisting it?

_____

_____

What will I do to prepare myself for what I fear?

_____

_____

How will fear serve me in areas I wasn't aware of before, because the fear itself held me back?

_____

_____

Now, let's welcome you to the next chapter, **Discipline**.

Chapter 7

Welcome to Discipline

"Discipline is the bridge between goals and accomplishments."
Jim Rohn

Discipline is defined as 'control gained by obedience.' The power of discipline is a magical creative force which sets you free, once you embrace it. I bet you have had some form of discipline in your life. Everyone has. The question is, in which areas of your life have you had discipline?

Some people perceive discipline as punishment and captivity. It is quite the opposite, discipline gives you freedom!

I was very well disciplined in the academic side of life. I set time aside daily to study when I was at high school and university. I stuck to my routine, and maintained my discipline. These days, I am disciplined in my vision for teaching personal development.

I have strong discipline when it comes to health and fitness, developed over years of seeing the positive benefits in my life. I often get asked, "How can you, man?" when I tell people that I run 5 kilometers at 6:00 am, in the dead of winter when it is cold, wet, and pitch black. My response is simple, "I do this through the power of discipline."

People who ask me, "How can you, man?" are under the impression that it takes a lot of effort to run at that time of the morning in winter. I am simply using the power of discipline to serve me. Yes, it serves a great purpose. If I am to list the benefits of running at that time of the morning, I would fill an entire page. I would say something along the lines of, "Running early in the morning gets my metabolism going, improves my blood circulation, I burn more fat, and it's a great mental start to the day, any day of the year!"

So, if discipline is serving me in such positive ways, why would I do anything other than use discipline to my advantage?

People who see discipline as something they would rather avoid, believe discipline will not serve them.

I have heard that many successful business leaders have a martial arts or military background! When I give that statistic to my corporate clients, I always ask them, "What one word comes to your mind when I give you that statistic?" Everyone that I have proposed that question to has said, "Discipline."

Discipline truly is a wonderful practice. People who master discipline know that there is far more to it than just the effort required to maintain it. If I could sum up discipline in one word, it would be 'rewarding.'

Yes, discipline is very rewarding, indeed. Look at your life, and ask yourself:

Where have I had discipline?

Then ask:

How has this discipline benefited me?

Even if you have to think for a moment or two, I'm certain you can answer these two questions. I truly believe that everyone has had some form of discipline in their lives. If you had discipline in the academic field, then you would have reaped the rewards of being an outstanding scholar. If you had discipline in maintaining your health and fitness, you would have reaped rewards of being fit and healthy. If you have discipline in your profession, then you would have had a rewarding career!

It is an irrefutable law of the universe:

Discipline = Rewards

Test this in any area of your life, and you would be proven right!

"Self-discipline begins with the mastery of your thoughts. If you don't control what you think, you can't control what you do."
Napoleon Hill

When I consult with clients who have started small businesses, I emphatically point out that discipline is needed to make their business grow. If I speak from that premise, I can safely say that discipline results in some form of growth.

I used to do weight training with my best friend, Gus, when I was in my early twenties. We both had discipline when it came to training, diet, and rest. Our discipline resulted in growth; the growth of muscles!

Or, let's look at someone who wants to learn how to play a musical instrument. She will be well-served if she implements a level of discipline which allows her to learn and practice the musical instrument she is interested in. If the discipline is well applied, she will become a better player. Her ability to play this instrument will grow.

You will grow in some capacity once you invite the power of discipline into your life. That is a given. I have seen it time and time again in my life and in the lives of people with whom I have consulted.

Whenever a client suggests that discipline seems like a lot of effort, I quickly question them, "What is the alternative then?"

If you ever think that discipline is too much of a price to pay, ask yourself this question:

What is the opportunity cost?

I learned all about opportunity cost when I was at university, studying economics. Opportunity cost implies "the lost opportunity." In other words, if I don't do this, what will I miss out on?

Every time I ask clients about opportunity cost, they gain clarity straight away that discipline requires work, and then the reward will come!

I have found that most discipline is simple to gain and maintain. Yet, some think it's complicated and way beyond their grasp. Discipline is within anyone's grasp. Any new parent will tell you he must be disciplined to look after his new child. Anyone with a new dog will tell you he must be disciplined in looking after his new dog. Anyone who has received a promotion at work will tell you he must have discipline in fulfilling the duties of his new role. The list goes on.

When I discuss discipline with my clients, I look for discipline they already have, or had, in any area of their lives! Then, I ask them to apply the same discipline from those areas, to the areas we are working on together. It's that simple. People who master it will tell you it is very simple once you understand and apply it. Discipline is a driving force which puts you in control of something that matters to you!

Understanding the reward in practicing discipline is just a matter of realizing that it serves a greater purpose, rather than punishing or keeping you in captivity. The power of discipline is obvious in the elite sports stars in our world. Do you think they get admired, adored, and paid millions of dollars by doing nothing? They apply the power of discipline and are rewarded handsomely!

> *"Self respect is the fruit of discipline;*
> *the sense of dignity grows with*
> *the ability to say no to oneself."*
> **Rabbi Abraham Joshua Heschel**

I once received a request from a young man who was going to court for an offense that he had committed. He did something in the spur of the moment, which got him to face the judge at court. He was a very pleasant young man, who was well-respected in the community. He wanted me to support him in court to ask the magistrate to give him a chance to prove himself, and to show that an isolated event does not necessarily define a person's character. I prepared a proposal to put him on a 10-week intensive coaching and mentoring program with me, where I would teach him to take full and absolute control of his life.

This young man was an accomplished amateur boxer, and had hopes of a career in boxing. He had a lot of discipline. This was obvious through his credentials in boxing. In court, I told the magistrate that I would support him to implement the same discipline he had in boxing, into other areas of his life. That is all this young man needed. He already had discipline; all he had to do was implement it, to take full control of his life.

The same applies to you. Use the discipline you already have and implement it in your life where you wish to grow more!

One thing that helps maintain discipline is accountability! When I first began life coaching, I told my clients that as their life coach, I would be their 'accountability buddy.' It really helps to have someone holding you accountable for the commitments you're making. As I mentioned earlier, when I was doing weight training, Gus was my accountability buddy and I was his. We maintained our own discipline and supported each other's discipline as well.

I strongly suggest you get an accountability buddy to create and maintain your discipline. Your close friends and family will love being your accountability buddy, to help you be successful. When I had a life coach supporting me, he was my accountability buddy. You could be wondering at this point, "Does a life coach need a life coach?" The answer to that is a resounding 'yes.'

My life coach was a great man by the name of Jay Mair. He really supported me in overcoming challenges I faced at a certain point of my life. His support drove me forward to achieve my goals.

One lesson I learned by using a life coach was how to be congruent in what I taught others. If I believed people needed life coaching, then what made me different from them? So, I had a life coach myself.

Discipline is needed as much in your professional life as it is in your personal life. With my corporate clients, I address discipline in their professional lives, and how they can use it to make changes in their organizations or respective careers.

A client of mine, who had started his own business, felt he needed discipline to plan his working day. The thought of being his own boss seemed very appealing at the start. However, he found that, in being his own boss, he did not have the discipline required to grow his business, so he started resenting the 'worker' in himself, because the desired results were not being produced! So, this particular client was ready to throw in the towel and go back to paid employment, because his new business was not generating the results he desired.

I spoke to him about implementing discipline in his work day and sticking to whatever was required of him. We structured his work days so that he had to stick to the plan to get the results he wanted, and I held him accountable to carrying out every task in his ideal week. I knew from the start that he needed discipline.

Within two months, his business started gaining momentum. He got more and more clients each week, and finally found himself in a much improved scenario from when he was ready to throw in the towel! In fact, during our last session, we discussed the absolute maximum number of clients he could see per week! His business was so productive that his ideal week had no capacity to accommodate new clients.

"The cost of regret far exceeds the price of discipline."
Dan Green

I wrote the article below in my newsletter (September 2009 edition), because I was inspired by the level of discipline showed by a man who had mastered it. I hope this article touches you like it touched the subscribers of my newsletter.

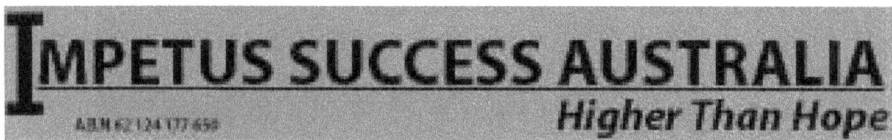

Greetings, and welcome to IDEAL INSIGHTS, a newsletter designed for people who are looking to make a positive difference in their lives.

The Power of Discipline.

I regularly train at a local boxing gym (in Melbourne's north), and recently I was fortunate enough to meet an amazing man, Mr Adrian Charter. Now, Adrian comes to the boxing gym to train, just like me. The difference is I am 31 years old and Adrian is 72!

I watched Adrian as he was training, early on a Sunday morning, and he was hitting the punching bag harder/quicker than most men in their twenties would! Later on that morning, I had a chat with Adrian, because I was very intrigued about his level of discipline.

You see, Adrian was a former boxer whose last professional fight was in 1968 (that is well over 40 years ago). Even though he has stopped competing as a boxer, his discipline still makes him stick to a very gruelling training regime.

It simply amazed me how a 72 year old man could train so hard, and believe me, boxing is one of the most demanding sports on Earth, requiring both aerobic and anaerobic fitness.

What surprised me even more was that a few days earlier, he did some running (and he ran for 9 kilometres). He does this on a regular basis. On a personal note, I run almost every morning, and when I do distance running sessions, I average approximately 5 kilometres per running session. So, Adrian certainly challenged my thinking when it comes to my own distance running sessions.

Adrian told me that his discipline was driven by what is in his mind. When I questioned him about how he maintained such discipline, he calmly replied, "It is all in my mind mate!"

So, I stopped and thought about it for a moment. If discipline can drive a 72 year old man to train so hard (and enjoy it), could I imagine how discipline could serve every single human being on the face of this planet?

Right at this point, as you read this newsletter, please pause and ask yourself, "What is my level of discipline in certain areas of my life?"

Discipline is defined as "Control gained by obedience." As a life coach and speaker, I often discuss the subject of taking control of our lives. The question is, can we take control of our lives without discipline? I strongly believe that discipline is needed to take control of anything.

Carefully analyze your level of discipline and give it a score or a rating, on a scale of 1 to 10. Then ask yourself, is this my true level of discipline?

A follow up question would be – can this be done better? By asking yourself that question, you will be constantly looking for answers to assist you in raising your level of discipline.

I will be emphatic on the word "constantly." It is said that success in any undertaking requires to constantly keep improving! The same applies to our level of discipline.

Once we have raised 'the bar' in terms of our discipline, our next goal or challenge will require us to once again improve our level of discipline! Hence, it is important to review and improve our level of discipline on a constant basis.

Sai Baba said that, "Discipline is the mark of intelligent living." I believe that every intelligent person values the importance of discipline.

Discipline sets you free from limitations that hold you back from achieving your goals or being at your best. Adrian is a prime example of how discipline can be used to achieve a goal (in his case, staying fit and healthy).

Discipline leads to more positive results. Discipline is a positive trait to have, and I would be inclined to say that positive traits attract positive results!

So, if you are to achieve a particular goal in your life, use the power of discipline. Implement and uphold a level of discipline that will serve you a very positive purpose in achieving your goal, or succeeding in any given aspect.

Just remember, at times discipline may require you to do certain things that may feel far from good or may seem very challenging. If you come across this, keep your focus on your end result and remind yourself that what you are doing through the aid of discipline will only serve you to achieve your goal. Adrian's wisdom told me that discipline will require us to push ourselves harder.

Regardless of how challenging it may feel at the time, the power of discipline (when implemented and applied correctly) will get you to the finishing line, and you will be handsomely rewarded!

It is said that if there is No Pain, there is No Gain. I say, the bigger the challenge, the greater our discipline can serve us, and the sweeter the taste of success!

So, come and join the Adrian Charters of this world, and claim freedom through the power of discipline.

> *"Success is nothing more than a few simple disciplines, practiced every day."*
> **Jim Rohn**

Wishing you all the very best.

Yours in Higher Inspiration,
Ron Prasad

| Impetus Success Australia | www.impetussucess.com.au |

As you can see from this newsletter, Adrian is driven by discipline. He had discipline in his youth as a professional boxer. Now, he uses the same drive to stay fit, healthy, vibrant and agile in his 70's! Adrian is truly an inspiration to be around! The boxing gym officially opens at 10am on Sundays, and Adrian likes to come early to train. I would purposely go to the boxing gym at 8am on Sunday mornings, because I knew Adrian would be there, training hard. Being around Adrian is very exciting indeed. I have a great deal of respect for this great man, who is a master of discipline.

I apply a high standard of discipline in my health and fitness. I exercise regularly, follow a vegan diet, and abstain from alcohol and cigarettes. This pays great dividends.

Vitality and ability are connected. The more vitality you have, the more ability you have! Your body is the physical vehicle that carries you in this life. Look after your body. Only allow healthy and productive consumables to pass through your lips. Exercise regularly, and see what difference it makes to your life.

The benefits of a healthy diet and regular exercise are so important. Medical or scientific research aside, common sense tells you it's wise to follow a healthy diet, and a suitable exercise program.

Are you in the right physical state to achieve your goals, and make the most of your life? Take control of your health, before it takes control of you! You can maintain a healthy diet, engage in some form of regular exercise (please consider medical advice before undertaking any exercise regime), and have a mindset which supports your health and physique. When people ask you how you have the energy to exercise so much, you can tell them that your vitality supports your ability! I have seen this over and over again, that people who are fit and healthy seem to be energetic and full of life! Please join them, and lead by example. In other words, inspire others by being inspired!

A healthy way of eating and regular exercise can give you an empowered mindset! You can plan your actions to handle a challenge when you are exercising. While exercising, you will feel more empowered, more vital, more able, and more alive!

> *"Man is made by his belief. As he believes, so he is."*
> **Bhagavad Gita**

Now, let's talk about discipline when it comes to using your thoughts and feelings about your goals.

Many personal development gurus know this concept, and have applied it to themselves and others in their lives. It is called their ideals! This is not my concept, I have learned it from masters in the field.

When refer to the word 'ideal,' I am not quite referring to the traditional definition, which is 'a standard of perfection or excellence.' I am referring to the word ideal, as explained below.

An ideal is an idea that you fall in love with! So, you put the 'L' for love at the end of the word idea and it becomes an 'IDEAL.'

When an idea comes to your mind, you consciously give it thought. You purposely think about that idea. Then once you fall in love with that idea, it becomes an ideal, and the ideal nourishes your thoughts.

Think back to a time when you took interest in a hobby. When you first discovered the hobby, the process of learning and honing the skill excited you. You became passionate about sharpening the skill and producing the best quality of product you could. You were no longer thinking about how to do it, you were taking action and making it happen, because it had become an ideal. An idea you loved.

Take, for example, writing poetry. Let's say you've always enjoyed reading poetry, and one day, you had an idea to write some of your own. You started reading through magazines and jotting down ideas and taking notes on how to put together different types of poems. After a while, you realized you had a true passion for writing poetry and it had become something you truly loved. Your idea about writing poetry as a hobby had become an ideal, an idea you loved. You weren't making an effort to think about writing poetry, it was something you just did. Your passion for writing it and improving your skills carried you through to your ideal, being a poet!

Please look at the illustration below:

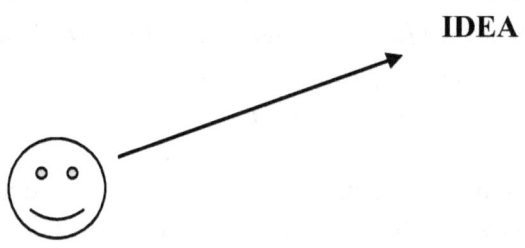

As you can see, an idea is what you give thoughts to. The arrows are your thoughts.

Then the idea becomes an ideal:

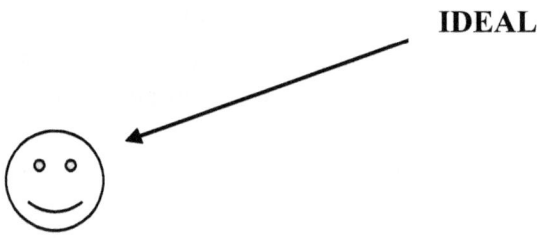

Now, the ideal is feeding your thoughts. You no longer have to consciously think about the idea, because the idea is now an ideal, it is automatically feeding your thoughts.

"We all have dreams. But in order to make dreams come into reality, it takes an awful lot of determination, dedication, self-discipline and effort."
Jesse Owens

Turning an idea into an ideal is a great way to achieve a goal. My idea was to write this very book. Then one night, Warren sat me down, and asked me to turn this idea into an ideal! There was no stopping me then! I fell in love with the ideal, the goal of excellence, in writing this book. I thought about how many people's lives could be changed for the better, once they applied the teachings of this book!

So, if you have a goal in your life right now, turn it into an ideal! Think about it with such intensity that the thoughts start feeding your drive to accomplish it automatically. Envision yourself having achieved that goal already! Use that feeling to build your ideal, your perfect example. If I can do it, so can you!

Do you have your notebook and pen handy? You can start getting excited and looking ahead when you address the questions below:

What is one goal that I would like to accomplish in the next 12 months?
How can I turn this goal from an idea to an ideal, an idea which excites you and motivates you into action?
What might happen if this goal becomes an ideal?

Please give some thought to the above questions. Once you understand the concept of ideals, you will be in control to achieve your goal!

"Meditation brings wisdom; lack of mediation leaves ignorance. Know well what leads you forward and what holds you back, and choose the path that leads to wisdom."
Buddha

Maintaining control of your mind, to stay focused on discipline and turning ideas into ideals, is given a boost by meditating. There are many forms of meditation. In the simplest sense, it means to go within and find your calm center. When you meditate every morning, it really puts you in control of your day.

Meditation has many benefits, including calmness, control, and connection. If you have meditated in the past, you would know exactly what I am referring to. If you are new to the concept of meditation, I would suggest that you explore this further. There are many great books and audio books on this topic.

I sometimes take clients through a guided meditation at the start of their life or executive coaching sessions. I have noticed these clients are more grounded and present during our sessions after the guided meditation.

I use a meditation technique taught by meditation master, David Morelli. The way David guides people to be centered, grounded, and receptive is amazing.

You can visit www.everythingisenergy.com to get in touch with David Morelli's meditation techniques. I have seen the benefits in many a client's experiences, and I strongly recommend it.

Welcome To Your Life

"Blessed is the man that You discipline, Oh Lord."
Psalm 94:12 NIV

Discipline is very helpful in your personal and professional life. If you are a business owner, you know what it takes to be disciplined, and how rewarding it can be.

I have a friend named Jeremy Huggins, who has his own web hosting business in web hosting (www.jnhsolutions.com.au). Jeremy promises his customers that he will respond to their inquiries within 24 hours, no matter what. He insists on that level of customer service, and his customers are very satisfied. I am one of them. There have been times when I needed Jeremy to assist me with my website at unreasonable hours, and he has delivered each time!

One of the biggest areas where discipline can serve your purpose is your self-image. Self-image is something that most people pay little attention to. Most people think and talk about self-esteem. Self-esteem is how you feel about yourself. Self-image is how you see yourself.

See the importance of self-image in John Kanary's quote, "You will never outperform your self-image."

It can take much discipline to maintain a self-image which serves your greater purpose and vision. Your self-image dictates the way the world sees you, so it is up to you to present yourself the way you want to be seen. Your self-image will enable you to get over hurdles when you are facing a challenge. Whenever you set a goal, see yourself as capable to achieve that goal.

I was once a guest speaker at an Aboriginal Youth Bush Camp. I started my speech by telling these youths the benefits of enhancing their self-image. I knew that at their ages, their self-image played a major part in their lives in how they saw themselves. Although the organizer of this camp wanted me to be a motivational speaker, I chose to speak about self-image instead, and share my insights with these youths. I shared John Kanary's quote with them, and they were moved by the power of the message.

Be disciplined and create the self-image that encourages and supports your ability to achieve your goals.

Another area of your life where you can see the importance of discipline is in giving. Giving makes us richer in every aspect of life. Consider scheduling into your time, a certain number of hours of volunteer work, or at least one volunteer activity, each month. As Tony Robbins has said, "We truly live when we begin to give!"

When you give your time to a worthy cause, you will find you have more than enough time for other things in life. Some of my corporate clients used to tell me they didn't have time. My question to them was, "What do you mean, you don't have time? Everyone has 24 hours in a day." If you do volunteer work, on top of your hectic schedule, watch how everything still fits into your schedule perfectly.

"To make it through those times, rely on the rock of discipline, not the shifting sand of emotion."
John C. Maxwell

The same principle applies to the discipline in donating money. I believe that giving to a worthy cause will give you more rewards than you can give away! I have found, through charity work, you will meet so many wonderful people. These are like-minded people who share the same passion with you, in making a positive difference in the world! Some of these people can become your close friends. Once you start giving more, you will feel more connected to your values. There is so much more to giving than what some people may initially think.

There is an animal sanctuary, north of Melbourne called Edgar's Mission (www.edgarsmission.org.au), where I volunteer. I support them financially as well. What I have found is that, regardless of how much work I have on my hands, or how hectic my schedule may seem, whenever I volunteer at Edgar's Mission, I feel at peace with time, and I somehow have the assurance that I will complete all of my tasks in a timely manner.

I recently joined forces with a very giving man named Paul Dunn. He has created a network B1G1 (www.b1g1.com), that businesses can join and donate to charities through. It is important to make a difference to those who are in need (people and animals included)! His work might even inspire you to do something similar in your own community.

I encourage you to apply these concepts of donating time or funds to a cause that is meaningful in your own life, and watch the wonders unfold. You will need discipline, yet the rewards are truly worth it.

The power of discipline is truly magical. Apply it to your life, and see what wonders it produces. Just remember, implementing discipline will be challenging. The challenge is a small price to pay for the rewards that you will reap.

Self Assessment

Which areas of my life need discipline?

_____

_____

How will I implement the required level of discipline in these areas?

_____

_____

How will discipline serve me in these areas?

_____

_____

Now, let's welcome you to the next chapter, which is **Gratitude**.

Chapter 8

Welcome to Gratitude

"In life, we should be happy with what we already have, and happier with what we will receive."
Anonymous

Gratitude is defined as the state of being thankful. I, for one, have been a big believer in the power of gratitude. I always believe that the more I express my gratitude, the more happiness I will have in my life.

Get your notebook ready and ask yourself at this point:

- How do I express gratitude towards others, the world, and God (or your higher power, if you believe in one)?
- What am I generally grateful for?
- How often do I express gratitude?
- Why am I grateful for these things in my life?

Answering these questions will connect you with the essence of expressing gratitude. The essence of expressing gratitude is being thankful with your thoughts and feelings. I have found, through years of experience, that expressing gratitude gives me an empowering feeling and also a better perspective on life.

Following on from the questions that you just asked yourself, please:

- Make a list of everything you are grateful for.

Make this list as comprehensive as possible. Ideally, spend 5 to 7 minutes on making this list! The idea is to encourage you to express gratitude from your inner being, without looking outside yourself for things that you should be grateful for!

Initially, list everything you are grateful for that comes to mind. Then, think deeper. List all the things you are grateful for, that perhaps you may take for granted. These are the things that are so common in your life that you don't usually think about how much of an impact they have. For example, you are fortunate enough to have clean, running water in your home, whereas others might not have access to clean water at all.

Think about these things. Bring them to the surface, and write them down.

Once you have made that list, read it. As you read each item on the list, pause for a moment and just absorb the gratitude. For example, one of the items on your list could be "I am grateful for the work that I do." Read that statement on your list, and absorb the gratitude by realizing the benefits of doing the work that you do. You can break it down in finer detail, and focus on even the little things that you appreciate about your work.

You can be grateful for your capabilities. Everyone is capable of doing something productive. If you consider yourself a good cook, then focus on the fact that people like eating what you cook.

You can be thankful for your immediate or extended family, such as your spouse, your children or your parents. Break it down into finer detail and analyze what makes you grateful for them. Is it because they always ask how they can help and give you unconditional love? Is it because they encourage you to move out of your comfort zone, or many other unique reasons? I'm sure you will have fun thinking about this and writing your list.

Take your time in absorbing the gratitude that arises with each item. Fully reflect on the reasons why you are thankful for each item on the list. Realize and reiterate what each item on the list means to you. Look at all the beauty in your life resulting from each item on the list.

Have a strong focus on this list, and take yourself through it every morning and night for 7 days. You must read this list with intensity, and absorb the gratitude. Do not make it a chore. Make it a loving ritual that you look forward to do. I can safely say that if you do this for 7 days straight, your outlook on life will be changed!

I once had a client who was feeling down after a break-up with his girlfriend. He was so bogged down with bitterness, resentment, and anger that he could not see any light or hope in life. He thought that his happiness had ended right there. They had planned a happy future and a family together. Then, she decided they were not a right match for each other just months before their engagement.

He told me that he could not accept her leaving. There were only negatives for him. He was completely focused on the loss of his girlfriend. He saw this loss as the loss of his happiness! I knew at that point he needed to understand the power of polarity, since everything has a polar opposite in life.

> *"What we appreciate, appreciates."*
> **Marci Shimoff**

To understand the power of polarity, I gave him some homework. I told him to:

Make a list of 100 things that he is grateful for, toward her.
Make a list of 100 things that he is grateful for, toward the relationship that he had with her.
Make a list of 100 things that he is grateful for, toward the break-up.

It took a lot of thinking and writing for him to do this exercise, yet he did and it worked wonders for him. Gone were the bitterness, resentment, and anger. These were replaced by gratitude. He was so grateful that he got to experience these things, thanks to her. He was also more grounded afterward. His entire outlook towards her, and the relationship, had changed.

To me, this seemed like a simple exercise, and I told him to keep it as simple as he could. He did just that.

Let me make one point very clear: expressing gratitude is not 'sugar coating' circumstances in one's life and just pretending to be happy and thankful. Expressing gratitude is a gift itself.

Expressing gratitude is a very empowering experience. Yes, gratitude makes you empowered. You come to the realization that there are many blessings in your life, and they can help you feel empowered and inspired!

The empowerment and inspiration from gratitude makes a difference in your attitude when you are facing adversity! Sometimes you don't see the gifts until after the situation happens. Remember the man I mentioned earlier who had lost everything during a major flood? He was thankful for his family being safe and well!

> *"Develop an attitude of gratitude.*
> *Say thank you to everyone you meet*
> *for everything they do for you."*
> **Brian Tracy**

Below is an article written by my dear friend, Keith Ready. It shows how gratitude can work wonders when expressed towards others.

Glowing and Growing with the Appreciation

The fact that I had taken time to congratulate him for his efforts was a seemingly small gesture from my point of view and took less than a minute to say, however, it had a big impact on his day, as he smiled and his face lit up in response to my short yet sincere comments.

It was clear to me that the personal and internalized pride he showed in a job very well done was something that was very important to him and I am sure he really had no expectations that I would take time out to say what I had just said.

My words of appreciation was something I felt privileged to say, simply because I was impressed with what he had done and it was a measure of someone who was and is prepared to put in that little bit extra to make a very big difference in his business. Immediately after my comments he thanked me, then asked me did I see anything he could do to improve and if so, how could he make it a reality in his business. I must admit at the time I was not focused on what could be improved, so I guess my answer that I could not see anything he needed to improve, other than to keep doing what he was, doing was of little help to him - but it was an honest not a dismissive answer.

As I left him to continue on my day of business appointments, I realized that not only had I made a difference to his day by what I had said, but the positive comment had also encouraged him to seek out ways to make his even business better. In addition to this it had also lifted my spirits and I felt great that he responded so positively and valued my feedback.

So often we find that our business and personal life is punctuated with reviewing what went wrong or what needs to be fixed that we miss the opportunity to lighten up and be uplifted by giving and sharing some positive feedback, even if it is to a relative stranger.

I am reminded of the very wise comments of an old friend, trainer and business mentor who said, 'always look for the opportunity to find the positive in what people do, then give them genuine praise and watch them glow and grow with the appreciation.'

He loved using acronyms in his work, as it allowed him to shorten phrases or groups of words and as he put it - 'anchor and reinforce his message in the minds of those he trained and mentored.' His acronym for his work in training people to value and appreciate what others do and help them to glow and grow was - A.C.S.D.S.R.

A bit of a mouthful I suppose, but it has stayed in my mind all these years even if I have from time to time forgotten about its importance and to use it. I am sure you are wondering what it means, so here is the full version - Always Catch Someone Doing Something Right.

I can see him now, standing in front of a group of managers sharing with them his formula for not only getting the best out of people and helping them to grow, but also for making your day just that little bit better. As he talked with them about the value in doing this, many would respond - 'but what do you say if they do something wrong.'

His reply was such a simple but profound one - 'everyone does something right, you just need to look for it, let them know you value and appreciate it, then it is much easier to address what they may have done wrong and the solution to correct it.'

In addition, he would encourage everyone that he trained or mentored to use A.C.S.D.S.R. constantly in order to enjoy the personal lift your get from doing it.

It is good to be reminded of this wonderful acronym which I know needs to be maintained as part of my daily life and not just used occasionally. This is something I have now remedied today, by making a daily note in my diary for the coming month to act on it. After 30 days of A.C.S.D.S.R. I am sure this rewarding and enjoyable part of my life will again become a positive and ongoing habit.

Written by Keith Ready, 2008
www.agiftofinspiration.com

Gratitude is a very powerful tool in enabling you to reach your goals. Hypothetically speaking, if you take a hundred steps to reach your desired end result, expressing gratitude after each step would make your journey easier and more enjoyable.

Imagine how it would feel to say, "Thank God or universe, I finished taking the first step. One down, ninety-nine to go." The same would apply to the second step, then the third, and all the way along to the very final step, where you would express the utmost gratitude for finishing the hundred steps to your desired outcome. Expressing gratitude along the way gives you more reasons to keep going, even when you are faced with challenges.

"Every time you are feeling grateful you are giving love."
Rhonda Byrne

I hope you realize the simple things in life are as much a blessing as the major or significant things. Express gratitude towards what you normally take for granted.

Let me give you an example. I clearly remember that there was a gas crisis in Melbourne in 1998. An explosion at one of the state's major gas suppliers, cut gas from most Melbourne homes for a few days. That meant no cooking on gas stoves and ovens, no hot water from gas water heaters, and no heating from gas heaters. This was only a month after winter, so it was still cold! It reminded me that things I normally took for granted ought to be appreciated at all times, not only when I don't have them.

When the gas crisis hit Melbourne, people realized how challenging life could be once the gas supply was taken away from them. The thing is, you should not wait for a crisis, disaster or an unfortunate event to happen before you begin to realize what your blessings in life are. If something that you normally take for granted is taken away from you, life would not be the same.

Each time you tend to stop appreciating something or someone in your life, ask the very important question "What would happen if this person or thing were not there anymore?" Answering this question can put you in a very gratitude-filled mindset.

*"Have gratitude for what you have.
Have faith for what you need."*
Anonymous

This morning as I drove to the track where I run, I heard on the radio that today is the National Day of Giving Thanks. In Australia, we do not officially have a Thanksgiving Day. The announcer on the radio station said today is the perfect opportunity to be thankful for everything in our lives. What a powerful message delivered by a radio announcer!!

Gratitude fills you up with inspiring energy. Being thankful can mean you are feeling happy at the time of expressing gratitude. Think back to a time when you were thankful for an unexpected act of kindness or a gift you received at a moment you didn't expect it. Now ask yourself, "Was it possible for me to feel sad and upset when I was expressing gratitude?" It is very difficult to feel sad when expressing gratitude. Being thankful makes you feel good about what you have.

You can express gratitude in any circumstance. Just look for something to be grateful for in every situation, and more opportunities will come to you.

The following is an article I wrote about how much gratitude I ought to express towards a situation where I had initially hoped for a different outcome. It was published by *InspirEmail, Good Gabble Magazine,* and *Arkansas Aging.*

Because the sun was shining

It had been raining Friday night and I woke up early on Saturday morning, hoping for more rain so I could wash my car. You see, I live in Melbourne, Victoria, a State in south eastern Australia where we have severe restrictions on water usage, so, I only wash my car when it is raining. I had a bucket, sponge, 'car soap' and umbrella at the ready. It had been quite a while since we had any rain and my car was extremely dirty and looked very neglected!

When I looked outside my window, the sun was shining and the rain had completely stopped. My hopes of washing my car in the rain were dashed. I stood outside, staring at my car and wondered what could have been. Then I noticed all the droplets of water on my car, shining in the radiant morning sunshine.

Right, there and then, it clicked - I could still wash my already wet car and then rinse it off with some rain water I had collected when it last rained!

So, time to get to work! The air was fresh, the sunshine was slightly warm and before I knew it, I had washed my car clean, all in the sunshine without an umbrella.

What's next, I thought? It is a sunny day, so, I had time to take my dog for a walk. He always loves to walk and enjoys the exercise and so do I. While walking, I said 'good morning' and smiled at a man who was mowing his lawn. I also said 'good morning' to another gentleman who was walking his dogs.

I could see my shadow and my dog's shadow on the ground, as the morning sun beamed upon us from behind.

I was totally oblivious to my so called 'dashed hopes' of washing my car in the rain. I kept patting my dog as we walked. He would look up at me and his eyes and face expressed his joy in being able to have an early morning walk in the sunshine.

Not an hour ago, I had woken up and felt overwhelmed with excitement to wash my car in the rain. Now, I was overwhelmed with gratitude at the priceless feeling of walking with my dog on a fresh sunny morning!

As I was walking back home, I saw a little puppy who stuck his nose out of the gate where he lived and wagged his tail at me. I gave him a pat on the nose. Then I saw my neighbour leaving home in his car. I waved at him and he gave me a wave back.

I got home and sat in the front porch soaking up the sun, whilst I reflected on the morning's events. I realized that, because the sun was shining:

I washed my car without an umbrella.
I enjoyed the fresh air and the warmth of the early morning.
I took my dog for a walk.
I said 'good morning' and smiled at a man who was mowing his lawn.
I said 'good morning' to another man, walking his dogs.
I said hello and patted a happy little puppy.
I waved at my neighbour as he left home.

While I was doing all of this, Bob Marley's classic . . . 'Sun is shining, the weather is sweet' 'kept ringing in my head. How appropriate, I thought! Had it still been raining, none of this would have been possible!

Had I been too hung up on the fact that the rain had cleared, it would have potentially set the tone for the rest of the day. Now, I had completely overlooked the fact that when I woke up, the rain had stopped, because all my energy and attention was centered on the joy I had experienced and the abundance of gratitude that I was feeling.

Clear blue skies, the sun shining just above the horizon, fresh air, a clean car, a happy dog and a grateful me - that was more than enough to send my spirits soaring to a much higher dimension!

Even on a grey day, it is important to remember that the sun is shining somewhere and it will shine on you in its own time. The key is to look for the best available opportunities, right there in front of you, and make the most out of them.

I had a great start to a great day, because the sun was shining!

Inspired by a sunny start to the day and written by Ron Prasad
Ron Prasad works as a Life Coach, when he is not washing his car in the rain, walking his dog and enjoying life.

InspirEmail © 2010

When I was interviewed by a radio station about this article, my message to the listeners was clear: "Find something to be grateful for, in every situation!"

> *"When you express gratitude for what you have, you'll get more of what you are grateful for. Anything we appreciate tends to grow."*
> **Dr. John DeMartini**

I was at a workplace Christmas party that one of my previous employers, one of Australia's largest financial services organizations, had organized. It was a warm summer evening and my colleagues were having a good chat over a few drinks and finger food. One of my colleagues brought up a few concerns he had about our workplace and suggested what could be done better. Then a few others joined in with their opinions. They all expressed their thoughts on what they did not like about working with this organization.

Each person made his point and suggested ways to make things better. We were all standing in a circle and chatting away as the night went on. This group of friends consisted of all young men, with a few years of experience in the workplace.

Then something happened which I will not forget until the day I die. One of my colleagues was listening in on the conversation, and had not said much until this point. He was a bit older than most of us and had many years of experience. He gently stepped forward and said "Boys, it could be worse." Those words hit me like a ton of bricks and I stood there motionless, absorbing what this friend of ours had said.

He went on to explain that we were all working in a corporate environment, sitting at comfortable desks, in an air conditioned (in summer) and heated (in winter) office with many modern facilities at our convenience. He then told us of his story in the workplace and how he started when he was our age. His first job was at a car assembly plant with a major motoring manufacturing company in Melbourne. His role was to stand all day long at an assembly line where the conveyor belt kept moving. He only had a few seconds to place the required parts on the motor, as the vehicle passed him on the conveyor belt. There was no time to do anything else, as the workers down the production line relied on him to get his job done right before they could begin theirs.

He reminded us that in our corporate workplace, we were at liberty to leave our desks and go to the kitchen to get water, tea, or coffee as we desired. We had the freedom to take a toilet break whenever we wanted. Such was not the case when he worked at the car assembly plant.

He went on to tell us about the working conditions. In our corporate office, the temperature inside the building was maintained at a constant level. In his role at the car assembly plant, the weather determined what the temperature inside the assembly plant would be. In summer, it could be extremely hot and in winter, it could be uncomfortably cold. Not to mention working overtime, which meant that he was on his feet for longer than standard working hours, while being subjected to the weather conditions.

I clearly remember taking his words to heart and suddenly being thankful for the job that I had at the time. I carefully analyzed every aspect of my job and expressed gratitude for what I had. Every time life throws a challenge at me, I remind myself of what this friend of mine had told me, "It could be worse."

> *"Having an attitude of gratitude opens up the channels for even more abundance to flow into your life."*
> **Jack Canfield**

Being thankful is a blessing in itself. Being able to realize the beauty in your life, and then expressing gratitude for it, is surely a blessing. Embrace that blessing.

This might seem a bit over the top, yet you can be thankful for simply being able to express gratitude itself. Learn from that blessing. Experience the empowerment that comes from being able to express gratitude. In other words, love gratitude, and love being able to express gratitude!

Expand and grow from that blessing. As you continue to express gratitude, you will be able to further expand your awareness from that blessing.

Look at the Special Olympics and Paralympics, for example. Regardless if competitors were impaired at birth, or as a result of an injury or accident, they train hard and compete at a top level with other great athletes. Their attitude determines their approach and therefore, what they can accomplish.

There was an advertising campaign a few years ago regarding people with physical impairments. I love the slogan of the advertising campaign which said, "A disability is a possibility." What a wonderful affirmation.

I believe that this statement does not only apply to people with physical impairments, it also applies to those disabled by patterns in their minds which hold them back from realizing their goals. Lack of confidence, lack of self esteem, feelings of inferiority, a sense of not being good enough, or thinking that "I cannot do that" are all similar to physical impairments if you take them on board. Look at Louis Braille for instance. He lost his eyesight at 3 years of age, yet he went on to invent a reading and writing system for the visually impaired.

Be grateful for every opportunity that life presents, even if the opportunity comes in the form of a challenge. The more gratitude you express, the more you will feel confident and assured.

I just read an article on Dan Caro, who was severely burned at 2 years old. Today he is the author of *The Gift of Fire: How I Made Adversity Work For Me*. He is also a talented drummer, and a motivational speaker. When I first contacted Dan, I could feel the positive energy that he so freely gives out to the world! I feel honoured to consider Dan a friend of mine!

It is people like Dan Caro and Louis Braille that accomplish great results, and pave the way for others!

"What we think about, and thank about, we bring about."
Dr. John DeMartini

Gratitude makes you more receptive. The more gratitude you express, the more receptive you become to new things to be thankful for. You will feel good about receiving, because you are now being grateful for what is happening to you, even if it's not what you expected. Please note that when I say "receiving", I am not implying what is served to you on a silver platter without any input or effort. I am making reference to receiving what you have earned and rightfully deserve.

If you find it challenging to be grateful during adversity, because it all seems so negative, I would suggest something small to you. Just ask "What lesson can I learn from this adversity?" Search for an answer. Once it comes to you, express gratitude for the lesson that you have learned in this adversity.

Years ago, I was driving a very standard car. Although it wasn't much to look at, I absolutely loved it. I had a daily ritual. Every morning when I parked my car at work, I placed my right hand on the hood of the car, and said, "Thank you for bringing me here." Although it was a very generic and standard car, I felt utmost gratitude towards it. It gave me years of driving, and I am still very grateful for it to this very day. Unlike some people who look at their cars as just a mode of transport, I expressed gratitude for having that car! Thanks to that car, I could travel to and from work.

Whatever you express gratitude toward, you connect with it in a way which makes you look at it in a different light.

> *"Appreciation is a wonderful thing:*
> *It makes what is excellent in others belong to us as well."*
> **Voltaire**

Be grateful for challenges in life. I have a friend who was just searching for a new job. When I asked him how he felt about his predicament, his response was "I am very excited about this new challenge that I am facing to find a new role." I found that to be a great formula to live by when facing a new challenge. You can get excited! Challenges present us with opportunities; let's be thankful for them.

One of my corporate clients just changed his whole business model. When I asked him how he felt about this, his response was, "I am really excited, mate!" I commended him for his amazing and empowering outlook.

Don't wait until you lose something important "You don't realize what you have until it is no longer there." Realize it NOW, not when it is no longer there! It is too late then. Expressing gratitude for what you had does not have the same meaning as expressing gratitude for what you have now. Fully cherish every beauty in your life. Go on a "beauty seeking" journey and find every beauty in your life. Do not leave any stone unturned. I can assure you there are things you have not thought necessary to express gratitude for.

Look around and see how you can value your life and all the beauty in it now. Do not wait for something to trigger gratitude in you. Do this right now. As I was saying, the more gratitude you express, the more inspired and empowered you will feel.

If things are looking completely out of control and there seem to be clouds of misery day in and day out, there is still hope. You might be on the verge of losing everything, yet there are always things in your life you can be grateful for. Michael Hill, is a prime example of this. He watched his house go up in flames when he decided to own his very own jewelry store. He then went on to create the mega chain of Michael Hill Jewellers!

You can look find things to be grateful for in every aspect of your life everywhere you go.

"Count your blessings and you'll soon lose count."
Anonymous

Live and breathe gratitude. Make it such a big part of your life that you can begin to encourage others to welcome and embrace gratitude in their lives, too.

Every day in my prayers, I say the following:

"Thank you, God, for everything that I was, everything that I am, and everything that I will be."

To end this chapter, I will leave you with one suggestion: Make gratitude a habit. Practice gratitude daily, then hourly, and whenever you feel like appreciating something. Then, you will find yourself expressing it without an effort.

Practice gratitude, especially when unexpected things happen. Remember to express gratitude then, too. You will be amazed at how your life unfolds when you discipline yourself to see good in truly every aspect of your life.

When something unexpected happens, ask yourself, "What lesson can I learn here?" Then express gratitude for the lesson. Open up to the universal forces and express gratitude in advance for what is about to come. Know that tomorrow, next week, next month, next year or in a few years time, this unexpected event will benefit you in some way or form! It is a very empowering feeling to be grateful for what is to come!

Make it an important part of your daily life and I can assure you that your life will seem brighter. Don't wait, APPRECIATE….

Self Assessment

How will I express gratitude from now onwards, at home, at work, and in difficult times?

_____

_____

How do I feel when I express gratitude?

_____

_____

How am I ready to use the power of gratitude to empower myself each day?

_____

_____

Now, let's welcome you to the next chapter, **Perspective**.

Chapter 9

Welcome to Perspective

"With a little perspective...
you can live a life of permanent purpose."
Jones (as told by Andy Andrews)

Perspective is defined as 'The aspect in which a subject and its parts are mentally viewed." We all have different perspectives about different things in our lives. Some serve us, some do not. The way that you mentally view something will determine how you feel about it! An empowered mindset leads to empowered feelings, so it is important to ensure that you have full control of your perspective at all times. Then you will be in a position to view something in a light which will give you an empowered mindset, and empowered feelings.

The whole purpose of writing this chapter is to allow you to take control of your perspective on someone or on something that currently does, or perhaps does not, serve you or feel good to you. Yes, your perspective is exactly that: yours. I often tell my clients that their feelings about something or someone have much to do with their perspective. They choose the perspective, consciously or unconsciously.

The good news is this: you can choose to change your perspective! Every one of us is in charge of our perspective. Some people just give in to what their perspective initially tells them.

I encourage you to take part in a little experiment. Just imagine this:

You are walking down the street on a busy shopping strip. It is Christmas time, there are Christmas decorations all around you, shops are playing Christmas carols, and there is festivity in the air.

Your hands are full, as you are holding shopping bags (recycled bags) with items that you have bought. All of a sudden you are approached by a very old, frail, sickly-looking person, who asks you for five dollars!

Welcome To Your Life

You feel fortunate to be in a financial position to do your Christmas shopping. It is the festive season, and you are inclined to give! Everyone seems happy and jolly. Five dollars is all that the person (who does not seem like he has long to live) is asking you for?

Then you give him five dollars out of your pocket! He says, "Thank you, God bless you," and then walks away.

Right now, please stop reading this book, and ask yourself?

What is my perspective of this situation?
What made me choose this perspective?

Please spend a few minutes in addressing these questions. It will give you a clearer understanding of how your perspective generally works.

Ok, now that you have addressed those questions, let us move on. Go back into the hypothetical scenario that I just gave you, and consider this:

You accept this person's blessings, and you wish him a Merry Christmas. He leaves, and so do you.

You feel good that you have done a good deed and put a smile on someone's face, especially during the festive season. You are also very receptive of the blessings that he gave you. You feel good!!!

Then you remember that you had to buy something else on your shopping list. You totally forgot about this. So, you make your way back into a shop, buy what you need, and leave.

As you walk through the shopping strip, you notice the same person sitting on the steps of an old building, smoking a cigarette!

Right now, please stop reading this book, and ask yourself?

What is my perspective of this situation now?
Why did I change my mind now?

"Perspective is an antidote to fear. Most things you fear will never happen, and even if they do, you can handle it."
Michael Josephson

Has your perspective about the situation, or this person changed? I would be very keen to know what you are thinking right now. The reason why I asked you to play with this hypothetical scenario in your mind is because it happened to me several years ago.

Just before Christmas in 2005, I was doing some shopping in the heart of Melbourne City. It was a Friday evening, daylight savings, summer time, and I had just finished work for the day.

A very old, frail, sickly-looking lady did approach me and ask for some money. She said she did not have money for dinner. I gave her ten dollars, because that was the smallest single amount of money I had at the time. She must have been in her 80's, very frail looking, walked with a limp, and had a hunchback. I truly felt sorry for her, and happily gave her ten dollars!

In Chapter 1, I mentioned an example where you might have felt differently as a child, than as an adult, if you donate money directly to people less fortunate than you are, knowing that some might spend the money on personal habits with which you disagree. This is the event that changed my perception. It challenged my morals to financially support someone's drinking and smoking habits.

As it happened, I did see her smoking a cigarette on the steps of an old church, a few minutes after I had initially met her. Initially, I was smiling from ear to ear, telling myself that I was a good person, here to serve others, and I felt good giving to the needy.

I felt so glad that this lady gave me her blessings. I love getting blessed! My perspective of the whole scenario was that I was in a good position to give, I loved giving, and saw no better way to spread the festive cheer, than to give to someone in need.

When I saw her with a cigarette in her hand, I was in shock! I stood there for a few seconds, and just stared at her. She did not see me, in the hustle and bustle of Christmas shopping. The little voice inside of me (whose counsel I never take) told me that I had just been fooled!

So, I quickly asked myself a question:

Would my perspective of the whole situation remain as it was initially, had I not seen her with the cigarette in her hand?

The answer to that question was a 'yes'. A very resounding 'yes'.

Then I asked myself another question:

Am I assuming anything here?

The answer to that question was also a 'yes'. I took myself through my assumptions – that she has purchased the cigarette with my money, that she was a fake, that I must've been fooled!

Then I reminded myself that I was in control of my perspective, regardless of what I saw. I could choose to focus on the fact that I gave with good intentions. I decided the best choice I could make is that I meant well, and I would hold onto that meaning!

That lady chose to smoke a cigarette, whether she bought it with her money, someone else's money, or mine.

I chose to see that my actions served a higher purpose, to God or to the universe! I found solace in that!

Now, you can make up your own mind, and choose your own perspective on the scenario I have described above. Just remember, no two people's perspectives will be the same. So, you would be wise to choose yours!

> *"We judge others by their behaviour.*
> *We judge ourselves by our intentions."*
> **Ian Percy**

I spoke about gratitude in the previous chapter. One thing I have learned, and shared with my clients, is having control of your perspective puts you in a position to have more gratitude.

If you constantly look at the choices you have in your perspective of something or someone, you will realize that certain perspectives put you in a better position to express gratitude, and feel more gratitude. For example, if a friend asks you for a small favour, you might initially think that you must go out of your way to help. If you were to change your perspective and tell yourself that you are grateful for the opportunity to help a friend, you will be in a position to express gratitude. I always feel very grateful when my friends reach out to me, and ask me for my help. I feel good being in a position to help them.

Now, please allow me to make one thing absolutely clear, when I mention perspective and gratitude, I am not referring to a simple, one-dimensional view of good and bad, as illustrated in the example of "The glass is half full, so let's rejoice!" or "The glass is half empty, so let's cry!"

It is so much more valuable than that. I mean, if you use the 'half full or half empty' glass example, that's a good place to start when choosing your perspective. Having said that, there is so much more to learn from that point onwards!

What I am referring to here is this, if two people were in the exact same predicament, and each had totally opposite perspectives, my question to each would be this:

Which person's perspective is more beneficial to him?

In other words, which person's perspective empowers him more?

The next time you are in a situation where you must choose a perspective, please ask yourself, "Which perspective would better serve my higher purpose?" Feel what your normal reaction is. Then step back for a moment and evaluate it. Does your automatic way of thinking, the way you have always reacted before, serve your higher purpose now?

If you think a particular situation you are facing has a dead end, look around and see if you can find another route. The following poem sums up perfectly how to look for an alternative route if you come across what seems like a dead end.

Keep Swimming

TWO FROGS FELL INTO A DEEP CREAM BOWL,
ONE WAS AN OPTIMISTIC SOUL,
BUT THE OTHER TOOK A GLOOMY VIEW,
WE SHALL DROWN HE CRIED, WITHOUT MORE ADO!

SO WITH A LAST DESPAIRING CRY,
HE FLUNG UP HIS LEGS AND SAID " GOODBYE"

SAID THE FROG WITH A MERRY GRIN,
I CAN'T GET OUT, BUT I WON'T GIVE IN,
I'LL JUST SWIM AROUND TILL MY STRENGTH IS SPENT,
THEN I WILL DIE THE MORE CONTENT.

BRAVELY HE SWAM TILL IT DID SEEM,
HIS STRUGGLING BEGAN TO CHURN THE CREAM,
ON TOP OF THE BUTTER AT LAST HE STEPPED,
AND OUT OF THE BOWL AT LAST HE LEAPT.

WHAT OF THE MORAL? TIS EASILY FOUND,
'IF YOU CAN'T GET OUT… KEEP SWIMMING AROUND!!!!!!

Anonymous.

The two frogs were in the same predicament. One accepted its fate as perceived through his gloomy view and the other was optimistic. Being optimistic, he did not accept his fate as being the end of his life. He chose not to give in and did all he could to get out of the deep cream bowl. Notice how he said "I can't get out, but I won't give in?" That is the attitude which is needed when you come to what seems like a dead end.

Neither frog desired being stuck in a deep cream bowl. One frog accepted this as a dead end, while the other looked around for an alternative route. The end result, as seen by both these frogs, is miles apart. One died by drowning and the other got himself out. He knew he had to work to get out alive. Hence, he put in the work by swimming for as long as he could. His swimming around the bowl paid dividends by churning the cream, which enabled him to climb out of the bowl and he leaped to safety. He did not accept to be drowned, because he did not see this as a dead end.

Although this poem is fictional, there is a lot to be learned from it. So, the next time you 'fall into a deep cream bowl', will you 'drown in the cream', or will you 'swim around until your strength is spent' and find a creative solution?

It is very easy to get caught up 'in the moment' so to speak, and look at things from a perspective that does not serve your greater purpose. Realize that your perspective is always in your control, and you can choose a perspective that serves your higher and greater purpose!

"Pointing out the comic elements of a situation can bring a sense of proportion and perspective to what might otherwise seem an overwhelming problem."
Harvey Mindess

Having a perspective which serves your greater purpose, puts you in a better space to face challenges in life and achieve goals. We all have challenges and can benefit from having at our discretion, a perspective which will allow us to overcome challenges.

When I mention 'greater purpose' I am referring to a purpose that will serve you and, in the process, others as well! It could be something important, or it could be simply to help one other person. Can you think of something you do, or have done, which serves you and others? For example, if your colleague is constantly asking you for help at work, and you are very busy with your own, you may initially feel like you are being disturbed, and it is getting a bit annoying. What if you change your perspective to, "This is great! I am getting a chance to help a colleague in need, and at the same time, I am refreshing my knowledge about work. This purpose serves me and my colleague."

When I look at animal activists who do volunteer work which serves themselves and others in the process, it gives them satisfaction, and is aligned with their values. By the same token, it serves animals as well!

> *"There are only two ways to live your life. One is as though nothing is a miracle. The other is as though everything is a miracle."*
> **Albert Einstein**

One of my aunties had come to visit us, from another state. She stayed the night. In the morning, I opened my email inbox, and saw there was a lot of work to be done for the day! I felt a little overwhelmed, and planned my day straight away. Well, the least I could say is that it would be a very busy and productive day for me, indeed.

I quickly had breakfast, and was washing my cereal bowl, while my aunty was at the dining table eating. I wanted to rush back to my computer and start the work that was pending.

As I was about to leave the kitchen, my aunty very kindly said, "Ron, can you please cut some fruits for me? Apples, grapes and bananas would be nice. Thank you, son!"

At that very instant, I thought, "Oh, if only my aunty knew that I have so much work pending!"

Then I quickly asked myself, "What perspective would serve me a higher and greater purpose?"

Believe me when I say this, the answer came to me straight away! I began to think about my childhood. I clearly remember, going to this aunty's house to visit her. She lived in a different city at the time. She would cook so much food for us, and top that off with delicious sweets for dessert! I really enjoyed visiting this aunty. She always looked after us so well!

So, my perspective changed and I remembered. When I was a little kid, this aunty cooked so much wonderful food for me. The least that I could do now was cut some fruit and serve it to her.

I became so at peace with myself. I did not rush getting back to my computer to start on the work that was pending. I told myself that a few minutes to attend to my aunty's request was time well spent!

Needless to say, I put more love and gratitude in the task of cutting up the fruit for her.

When I served her the pieces of fruit in a bowl she said, "Thank you. God bless you." Those words were priceless.

I was in a much better frame of mind after I gave my aunty what she had so kindly requested from me. I expressed gratitude to God for the opportunity to serve my aunty early in the morning.

Then, when I did start working at my computer, I was functioning much better, because my perspective had allowed me to serve a greater and higher purpose! Long live my aunty!

> *"If you want to study yourself — look into the hearts of other people. If you want to study other people — look into your own heart."*
> **Friedrich von Schiller**

You can learn from the above story that having a perspective that serves a higher and greater purpose is at your disposal all the time. You can reach it by asking simple questions such as:

What perspective would serve me a higher and greater purpose?

Once you make it a habit to ask these types of questions, you will automatically start having a perspective that will serve your higher and greater purpose.

I am sure you can come up with other questions that will help you to nurture a perspective that will serve you better. Play around with this concept and see what else you can come up with!

I would like to share another story with you.

My little nephew was three years old at the time. One day, I was to look after him for a few hours. Now, he was a very active child who kept me on my toes.

A few days earlier, a personal development website had requested that I write an article for them.

So, that morning, I wrote on my to-do list "write article." By the time my little nephew arrived, I had done some other work, and still needed to write the article.

I played with him for a while, and then put on his favourite cartoon show, hoping he would enjoy the cartoon, and I could write the article meanwhile. That did not work at all. He wanted to come and play on my computer. I repeatedly told him that the computer was for work only, and he could not play on the computer.

He was very persistent and wanted to play on the computer. It got to a stage where I turned the computer off, and there went any chance of writing the article!

So, I told him that we could go outside and play with the doggy, or we could play with his toys. Guess what? He wanted both!

We went outside and played with his toys while my dog sat next to us, watching us play.

In the back of my mind, there was only one thought, "Write the article, write the article, write the article."

I could've chosen to see the scenario as "I am being disturbed; I am being annoyed; I am wasting my time". Then I asked myself a question, "What perspective would serve me to make the most out of this situation?"

The answer came. I could be in this beautiful, present moment and express my gratitude for being able to play with a child and give him happiness! I did just that!

It was amazing how my perspective made the situation feel even better. Every few minutes, my little nephew would put his toys on the ground, and say, '"Hug," while giving me a hug! Now, that is priceless.

So, I was just so glad and grateful to be spending time with my nephew and my dog, while feeling so much fulfillment!

As you can see from the above story, having a perspective that serves a higher and greater purpose could also provide me with fulfillment. I felt so much fulfillment while in the presence of a child and a dog!

Oh, by the way, I wrote that article later in the day, after my little nephew left!

"See the world with different eyes each day. Things barely change, the way we see things change."
Ronny K. Prasad

Perception is projection. The way we see the world is how we present ourselves. If we see the world as a beautiful place, then we will present ourselves as happy and positive.

The next time you are faced with a scenario where you can choose a perspective, ask yourself the following questions (in this order):

What is my current perspective of this scenario?
What perspective would serve me a greater/higher purpose?
What one or two things could I change to get that perspective?

The last question is easy to answer! Once you answer the second question, the answer to the last question should easily follow.

I sincerely hope that I have given you some insights on how to create a perspective (in different circumstances) which will serve you better.

Self Assessment

In what area of my life, can I begin to choose a perspective that serves a greater purpose? At work, with my family, or in my personal relationships?

_____

_____

What will improve in my attitude, when I change my perspective in this area? (What will improve, become easier, flow more freely?)

_____

_____

What will improve in my environment when I operate from a perspective that serves my greater and higher purpose?

_____

_____

Now, let's welcome you to the next chapter, **The Perfect Order**.

Chapter 10

Welcome to the Perfect Order

"There are no mistakes in the universe."
Dr. John DeMartini

Take this to heart. It bears repeating, and it begins the most important lesson of all. There are no mistakes in the universe.

When I first heard this quote, I only slightly resonated with it, because I had heard "everything happens for a reason." I thought, "Yeah, Dr. DeMartini could be right. Maybe everything does happen for a reason." At that time, I had read a number of great books in the area of personal development, and I knew that every life event served a higher purpose, whether in that very moment, or in the future. It had never occurred to me that I was actually part of this context!

This understanding, that my life was part of this perfection, too, began awakening within me. I kept repeating to myself, "There are no mistakes in the universe; there are no mistakes in the universe." The more I repeated it, the closer I felt that I got to fully realizing it!

That is my mantra now, and it just keeps proving itself right over and over again! I have so many stories I could share with you

Once this statement became my mantra, I started consciously observing my life, and evaluating everything that had ever happened to me. Slowly, I put the pieces of the puzzle together, and Dr. DeMartini's quote became firmly ingrained in my awareness!

Once I understood that there were no mistakes in the universe, my whole life started to make sense to me! I looked back at my life, and realized everything I had ever gone through was part of the perfect order!

You are a part of the perfect order, as much as I am! The perfect order is available to you right now. All you have to do is realize it.

I have noticed that when things 'don't go right' most people get angry, upset, or feel resentment, and in the process, they block themselves from realizing the perfect order.

Allow the perfect order to do its job in situations that may initially seem unfavourable.

If you used to get frustrated when you did not get what you wanted, when someone turned you down, or when you felt like you had 'lost' something, realize the perfect order is at work!

When I first began my own business in life coaching and motivational speaking, I approached people and organizations to show them the value in what I could provide to them. I knew that some people and organizations would not be receptive to what I offered. At times, it was challenging to get knock back, after knock back. I just kept telling myself this was part of the perfect order!

I knew the clients I was looking for were looking for me at the same time. It was just a matter of time before we met!

Early in my coaching business, I had a client who was in the same situation as I had been. He had commenced his own business, and was feeling the challenges of marketing and finding new clients. I took him through the perfect order, and left it up to him to believe in it or not.

He was a little skeptical at first. Then, once he began to believe in the perfect order, he noticed the people who knocked his services back were never really his ideal clients. I had been in the same position as he was when I commenced my own business. So, I understood the relief and gratitude he felt when he had this realization.

Another client, Kane Hammond, who has now become a very dear friend, so loved the concept of the perfect order that he began sharing Dr. DeMartini's statement with his family, friends, and friends. It is quite common for him to send me a text message at 6:00am with the words "There are no mistakes in the universe."

Kane started living his personal and professional life from the premise that there are no mistakes in the universe! Guess what? Proof of this comes to him every single day in various forms. All he had to do was realize it! He loves celebrating the fact that there are no mistakes in the universe.

I encourage you to celebrate the fact that there are no mistakes in the universe! All you have to do is look at the hidden gifts or blessings in what may initially seem like something unwanted or undesirable. Just keep an eye on the previously hidden blessings and gifts the universe is revealing to you!

In the western world, we tend to live by the clock. So, if we are a minute late for something, some people tend to take it as though all hell has broken loose! Every time that I am running behind schedule, or someone with whom I have an appointment is running late, I look for the hidden gift behind it.

One morning, my dear friend Kane, the director of his organization, was to meet me at his corporate office. He was behind schedule and I was waiting for him at his office. He called and asked me to come outside his office, and meet me in the car park, so he could drive me to a local cafe, and we could have our session there. I quickly told myself that there was a hidden meaning for Kane to be behind schedule and for the meeting location to change.

As soon as I left his office, I walked past a lady who looked familiar. I took a second look at her, and realized it was the exact lady whom I had been looking to contact for months! Her name is Patricia. She is 72 years old, and sings for The Choir of Hope and Inspiration. I had written an article about how inspiring she was a few months prior, and I had misplaced her phone number. So, I really wanted to contact her. Then, the universe just presented Patricia to me, through Kane being behind schedule! The fulfillment that I felt was beyond words! Kane saw me hugging Patricia and as soon as I walked up to him I said, "There are no mistakes in the universe!" Needless to say, we both laughed!

At times people tend to get carried away by the surface appearance. All they have to do is look for the hidden gift or blessing. Can you imagine if I became angry at Kane for not being at the meeting on our scheduled time? How would that have that served me, or Kane, for that matter?

"There are no mistakes. The events we bring upon ourselves, no matter how unpleasant, are necessary in order to learn what we need to learn; whatever steps we take, they're necessary to reach the places we've chosen to go."
Richard Bach

I sometimes laugh at myself when I realize how I reacted in the past when things did not go my way. I got so caught up in the moment that I missed the joyfulness in expecting what was to come. My expectations were low because life seemed to be working against me, until gradually my awareness shifted and opened up.

Dr. Deepak Chopra quotes in his book, *Synchro Destiny*: "When you live your life with an appreciation of coincidences and their meanings, you connect with the underlying field of infinite possibilities. This is when the magic begins."

Yes, magic it is, indeed. Whether you call it a miracle or magic, the perfect order will deliver it to you!

In my professional life, there have been instances where I felt I was hard done by, especially in job interviews. I doomed myself to thinking I would never get a job where I was completely fulfilled! I kept expecting things to go downhill in my professional life. I was conditioned to negative thinking and I always blamed other people or circumstances! That was until I heard the words from the master himself, Bob Proctor:

"I am responsible for my life, my feelings, and every result I get."

Upon hearing that quote, I realized that my professional life was unfulfilling because I never looked inside myself to decide what I really wanted. I didn't make changes that would lead me to a fulfilling career. I didn't realize that life had already prepared me with many of the skills I needed to become an entrepreneur. I just needed the realization that once I had the courage to strike out on my own path, the rewards would be tremendous.

One of the turning points in my financial planning career happened when a client came to me for some financial advice.

He was a refined and professional gentleman, in his 50's. He was looking at retiring, and wanted to know his retirement planning options.

As I completed the fact-finding documents with this gentleman, I discovered he was a very wealthy man, who held a senior position at one of Melbourne's universities. Furthermore, he lived in a million dollar property on an acreage in one of Melbourne's most affluent outer suburbs.

He was very soft spoken, humble, and referred to me as Mr. Prasad. I was really impressed by his humility, because he was almost double my age, and had quite a respectable social status!

He then started telling me about his humble beginnings, and how he made himself successful professionally and financially. He said to me, "You have to be successful in areas of life that matter most to you." In his case, it was the professional and financial side of life that mattered to him. Listening to him, I realized that I had so much to learn from this man. Those profound words were the greatest advice he gave me. Be successful in areas of life that matter most to you.

I quickly ran a check in my mind of what areas of my life were important to me. I noticed I needed to create more changes in certain areas of my life! I realized that being happy is very important to me. Being incongruent meant not being happy!

I have been very emphatic on congruency all my adult life. One of the things that really hit me hard was, there I was, talking to someone much more financially successful than I was, and I was giving him advice on financial matters. Is that being congruent? I had always believed in leading by example, and by practicing what I preached.

I realized that I was not being congruent with my values by handling other people's large amounts of money when I did not have large amounts of money at the time!

Logically speaking, I could have gone on with my financial planning career, advising people who were wealthier and older than I was. I was in my late twenties at the time and it was part of the profession to give advice to people who needed a financial planner, regardless of my age.

I thought back to another time, when I was a presenter at a retirement planning seminar. This particular seminar was for people who were looking at retiring within the next two or three years. The venue was full of people in their fifties and sixties. My manager, Cathy, was kind enough to be there with me. She was in her thirties at the time. We were the youngest people there. When I started talking to the audience, I heard someone whisper, "He is so young, what would he know about retirement?" I smiled at this lady's comment. I spoke for about an hour, and explained certain retirement planning strategies to the audience. They asked me questions, and I clearly addressed each one. I felt that I did convince the audience I knew about retirement planning, regardless of my age!

I kept thinking about what my distinguished financial planning client had said to me, to be successful in areas of life that mattered most to me. Then, I linked it to the retirement planning seminar. I had the technical knowledge to advise people about wealth building and retirement planning, yet I was neither wealthy, nor retired! This particular client really made me question my profession.

Initially, I felt shattered. I thought that I was being unfair to my clients, and I was being unfair on myself. I started thinking seriously about changing careers!

"Everything happens for a reason. Nothing happens by chance or by means of luck. Illness, love, lost moments of true greatness and sheer stupidity all occur to test limits of your soul."
Anonymous

Then along came some great advice from my dear friend, Siba Abdelki. She suggested that I consider a career in teaching personal development! She pointed out how I had used personal development teachings on myself and with my friends. So, she suggested I could transfer the knowledge onto my clients! The relief that I felt was overwhelming. I felt I would be congruent with myself and with my clients, if I taught personal development and initially became a life coach. That was the beginning of my journey of teaching personal development to live an empowered and inspired life!

The best part about this was that I felt totally congruent with what I was doing! My motto is simple:

> Inspire by being inspired!
> Empower by being empowered!

Once again, it was proven to me that there are no mistakes in the universe! I was feeling career unfulfillment for a reason. It all led me to my ideal career as a personal development teacher.

That was just one of the valuable lessons that I learned, as part of the perfect order.

Your search for the perfect order will continue to reveal itself, as you allow it to. One of my clients noticed in his personal life, there were times when he would show interest in a girl, and she would not respond. He began to see this as part of the perfect order, instead of seeing it as simply being rejected by a girl.

I shared with him a quote which said, "Rejection is God's protection".

This quote hit home with him, big time! He realized that every girl who rejected him as a potential partner, every employer who had rejected him as a potential employee, and every organization that had rejected him as a potential personal development trainer, did so because God was protecting him from something!

Welcome to the perfect order!

"The law of equilibrium serves you all the time. Every part of you equilibrates with all other parts of you. When you embrace your 'all-ness,' you become truly authentic."
Ronny K. Prasad

To further illustrate the perfect order in action, please read the story below written by my very dear and close friend, 'Lucky' Phil Evans. This story was featured in Bob Proctor's *Insight of the Day, Friday Story*.

This is Good

The story is told of a king in Africa who had a close friend with whom he grew up. The friend had a habit of looking at every situation that ever occurred in his life (positive or negative) and remarking, "This is good!"

One day the king and his friend were out on a hunting expedition. The friend would load and prepare the guns for the king. The friend had apparently done something wrong in preparing one of the guns, for after taking the gun from his friend, the king fired it and his thumb was blown off. Examining the situation, the friend remarked as usual, "This is good!"

To which the king replied - "No, this is not good!" and proceeded to send his friend to jail.

About a year later, the king was hunting in an area that he should have known to stay clear of. Cannibals captured him and took him to their village. They tied his hands, stacked some wood, set up a stake and bound him to the stake.

As they came near to set fire to the wood, they noticed that the king was missing a thumb. Being superstitious, they never ate anyone who was less than whole. So untying the king, they sent him on his way.

As he returned home, he was reminded of the event that had taken his thumb and felt remorse for his treatment of his friend. He went immediately to the jail to speak with his friend.

"You were right," he said, "it was good that my thumb was blown off." And he proceeded to tell the friend all that had just happened. "And so, I am very sorry for sending you to jail for so long. It was bad for me to do this."

"No," his friend replied, "This is good!"

"What do you mean, 'This is good'? How could it be good that I sent my friend to jail for a year?"

"If I had not been in jail, I would have been with you, and not here with you right now."

In a very unusual way, the message here unfolds into exposing the following principle about life.

"Absolutely everything happens for a purpose; and out of what seems like adversity at the time; always comes good".

I'm sure that if any of us care to reflect back on the tragedies, the heartaches, the 'bad times' in our lives, that we discover that we have really grown or developed during that period of time: even though the reflection may still cause us discomfort in some way.

It is in this way that we slowly gather experience and wisdom, and even though we may think or feel that it is unfair, that's the way it is.

"This is good". Many of our life's experiences have saved us from some form of cannibals; it's just that we often don't know that they have at the time.

So, for a simple example to help with awareness: next time you may begin to feel you are being 'wronged' by being stuck in a traffic jam, think about the cannibals that could be lurking down the road a bit, but will be gone by the time you get there.

Now that's a bit different, but worth trying: "this is good" - despite the circumstances.

© Phil Evans
www.peoplestuff.com.au

Welcome To Your Life

"The universe is always supporting you."
Marci Shimoff

The perfect order was further instilled in me once I ready Marci Shimoff's best seller, *Happy for No Reason*.

She clearly explains that the universe is supporting you all the time and everything is working according to this plan!

You can take this premise and start thanking the universe for always supporting you, regardless of what was happening. At times, people will say, "That is so bad," when you tell them what just happened. So, keep your firm belief that the universe is always supporting you.

The more you hold this belief, the more you will feel that the universal forces are your friends, here to support and serve you. What could possibly work against you, if all the universal forces are working for you?

What seems like 'bad' or 'against' you is all part of the perfect order the universe is using to support you! It's possible to feel in every cell of your body that you can achieve all your goals because the universe is supporting you!

One effective way to accept the perfect order is to express gratitude when things seem to go in a direction you had not desired! I mentioned the power of gratitude previously, and by now you know how powerful gratitude is.

When you come across a situation where things turn out as the total opposite of what you had hoped for, express gratitude! Yes, this may sound challenging to begin with. Start practicing anyway. You have so much to gain by doing so, and little to lose.

I do this on a conscious level all the time. For example, I once submitted a proposal to teach personal development at a youth center. The management of the youth center advised me that my services were not needed. I emphatically expressed gratitude for the youth center not accepting my proposal, because I realized the perfect order was taking its course! I knew that this was happening for a bigger reason. The more grateful I am, the more the perfect order shows up in my life in various forms.

As I mentioned, this can and will be challenging at times. Focus on the perfect order, and express gratitude for whatever has happened. Then, the perfect order will reveal why this event or circumstance has taken place. It will be revealed even if you do not express gratitude. If you stay in a mindset of gratitude, you will receive the lessons more easily, instead of being frustrated by outward appearances. Having said that, if you express heart-felt gratitude, no matter what the circumstance, the perfect order will seem to come into your life more emphatically!

I spoke about awareness earlier in this book. By now, you know how to expand your awareness, and use it to your advantage. The same awareness can be used to look for the perfect order in your life. I believe that the perfect order is an irrefutable law of the universe. It is here and will always be. Allow your awareness to embrace the perfect order of life, and just watch how it reveals its wonders!

Even when things seem to go really downhill, keep reminding yourself that it is here to serve and support you by letting you live according to your purpose! I have developed a habit of laughing and seeing the funny side of things, if something does not go as I have hoped for. I get excited, because my awareness tells me the perfect order is coming to serve and support me. What more could I possibly ask for? When I know I did what I felt was required of me, why would I get upset or caught up in the moment? If the outcome is not exactly what I had hoped for, my job is to let the perfect order reveal the plans of the universe to me.

"Everything in life is a lesson or a gift."
Kerry Riley

Exercise

Look back at a time when you felt at a loss because something turned out differently from what you hoped. Then address the following questions:

What did you initially think when the situation didn't work out?

_____

_____

Did you express gratitude at the time?

_____

_____

How did things turn out eventually?

_____

_____

Are you at peace with that particular situation now?

_____

_____

If you look for the perfect order in that situation, what will you find?

_____

_____

Are you grateful for that situation now?

_____

_____

Take your time in answering these questions.

Upon completing that exercise, please ask yourself what you discovered. Make a complete list of everything that you discovered as a result!

_____

_____

_____

_____

_____

_____

_____

_____

_____

_____

You can apply this exercise to any situation you have experienced, or any situation that you will go through in the future.

"I might not have control over everything that happens to me.
I can always decide how I accept it,
and how express gratitude toward it."
Ronny K. Prasad

Welcome To Your Life

I wrote this newsletter, about the perfect order. I hope you get something valuable from it.

Greetings, and welcome to IDEAL INSIGHTS, a newsletter designed for people who are looking to make a positive difference in their lives.

No Mistakes in Life?

On 24 June 2010, history was created in Australia, as the nation welcomed its first ever female Prime Minister, Julia Gillard. Indeed, this day was marked with celebration from men and women alike, for creating something which took 108 years. Women in Australia were first permitted to enter the political arena in 1902.

Let us focus on a massive change in Australia, when a woman became the leader of the country.

Going by Ms Gillard's story, I remembered the great words spoken by human potential expert, John DeMartini, who said "There are no mistakes in life."

Similar words were spoken by self development expert, Warren Henningsen, when he said "There is no such thing as a good experience or a bad experience. There is only experience." I loved this description because it removes any attachment to an experience.

I had the privilege of meeting with John and Warren last week. They are regarded and respected as insightful teachers of universal laws, which brings me to Ms Gillard's story.

Julia Gillard was born in Wales, and as a child had a medical condition called bronchopneumonia. Medical advice was sought by her parents and, as a result, they immigrated to Australia, in search of a warmer climate.

Now, if you are not well read in the area of mind dynamics or if you are not attuned to the universal laws which govern us, chances are that you may be inclined to view any medical condition as something of a negative.

Great teachers of universal laws will tell us that everything is happening in perfect order. It is up to us to be aware enough to look for the perfect order. Too often, people get so caught up in looking at the smaller picture, that they overlook any positives in what may initially seem like a negative situation or outcome.

Had Ms Gillard not been susceptible to bronchopneumonia, chances are that her parents would not have moved to Australia. What initially could have looked like a negative situation made the Gillard family to immigrate to Australia, and today, their daughter has become part of this nation's history.

I have read many accounts of people's stories where they were faced with hardship in health, relationships, career or finance, and yet they turned things around to their advantage. There is no shortage of such people on earth. I believe that these people are here to teach us a lesson, and give us a gift of hope, encouragement, empowerment, inspiration.

I have worked with clients who faced challenging situations, and then have moved forward to achieve greater results. I always tell my clients to stay away from putting labels on situations, such as, "This is bad" or "This is horrible".

One suggestion that I will make to you is this. When you are faced with what seems like a negative situation, please replace the word 'negative' with the word 'challenging'.

Instead of saying "I am facing a negative situation," tell yourself, "I am facing a challenging situation."

Which of the two statements sounds more empowering?

So, the next time you are faced with something seemingly negative or unwanted, please pause for a moment and ask, "What is this situation telling me?" Then ask "How could this situation serve me better either today, tomorrow or anytime in the future?" Another empowering question is, "Where could this lead me to?" Just look at Julia Gillard to find the answer to that question!

The Law of Polarity dictates that there is a positive for every negative. I now assign you the task to consciously live through that law.

After reading this newsletter, please ask yourself the following questions:

How do I normally respond to a situation which seems negative?

How could I possibly change my view to replace a negative problem with a positive challenge?

How will it serve me if I were to look for challenges in any seemingly negative situation, and then overcame the challenge to achieve greater results?

> "Every adversity, every failure, every heartache carries with it the seed of an equal or greater benefit!"
> **Napoleon Hill**

Yours in Higher Inspiration,
Ron Prasad

Impetus Success Australia   www.impetussucess.com.au

> "Feedback is the breakfast of champions."
> **Ken Blanchard**

I have noticed the perfect order can reveal itself in the form of feedback from other people. When people get feedback, most tend to put it into two categories, negative or positive.

I operate on a different premise. I believe that all feedback is there to help us, regardless of how it seems negative or positive. All feedback is helpful, without labelling it 'negative' or 'positive'.

If someone says something 'good' about you, generally you are elated and see yourself as being good at something. However, if someone says something 'bad' about you, generally you feel deflated and see yourself negatively.

The perfect order is there to equilibrate both the 'good' and the 'bad' feedback. That is what the perfect order does. Have you ever noticed how you feel when someone says something which makes you feel proud or delighted, and then someone else makes you doubt or question yourself? The interval between the two may be hours, days, or weeks. It is normal that your feelings will be elated and deflated in certain areas of your life. I feel elated about my mindset. I feel deflated about computers and technology because I know very little about them.

Look for the perfect order every time you are given feedback.

When I became a public speaker, I was very happy with the way, I spoke in front of people. I had joined Toastmasters International to sharpen my skills. I knew I was an acceptable speaker, yet I wanted to get better. Somehow I felt I needed the 'X factor' in my abilities as a speaker.

So, I started asking for feedback. After every speaking engagement, I would pass around a feedback form to the attendees, to get their feedback.

I was initially shocked to read some of the things that people said about me. Then, I would remind myself the perfect order was revealing itself to me, in the form of this feedback. I loved the feedback people gave. On the feedback form I would ask, "What are your suggestions for improvement?"

That opened the floodgates of ideas flowing to me! I was humbled by some of the wonderful things people said, and grateful for what others suggested I do to improve!

Needless to say, it was wise not to take the counsel of everyone who gave me feedback. What some people suggested would have been inappropriate in my opinion.

To all the businesses owners with whom I have consulted, who operate at a retail level, I have given one simple suggestion: "Please put a feedback box at the counter or customer service area. It opens up dialogue with the customers, and it shows you care about them."

What the feedback tells you is all part of the perfect order!

So, the next time you are given feedback, be it seemingly negative or positive, look for the perfect order in the feedback. You will operate from a different premise once you do that!

> *"Challenges are required for growth."*
> **Anthony Robbins**

Every challenge is part of the perfect order.

I like the way Wallace D Wattles put it: "The object of all life is development." Can you imagine what it would be like to live a life without any opportunity for improvement? If it was simply smooth sailing all the way and you were living in a comfort zone, the impetus for change, growth, improvement and development would not arise. It would be a very mundane and stagnant existence.

Challenges are part of the perfect order. Hence, challenges are here to serve you!

I came to the realization that:

A challenge is an opportunity which leads to a reward.

When I was undertaking my course in life coaching, I worked full time and most evenings were filled with homework and my fitness regime. Weekends were spent with family, friends and self-education. I realized that undertaking the course would be challenging and that facing the challenge was an absolute must to achieve my goal to become a qualified life coach. When I received my certificate which deemed me a qualified life coach, the sacrifices of evening classes, assignments and reading materials on the weekends, and the cost of the course paid big dividends.

Just remember one thing: No problem is big enough, a solution always reaches far enough! When I adopted that sort of thinking, my so-called problems in life seemed like a challenge that I could face.

The challenge, opportunity. and reward are all part of the perfect order!

Often people will lament over something they have lost. Many see loss as a major negative, and they spend much time and energy focusing on the losses.

The 'loss' is part of the perfect order.

In physics, there is the Law of Entropy, which is also widely known in the personal development movement as The Law of Vacuum The Law of Vacuum states that when there is a 'loss', a vacuum is created. According to this law, the higher power (whether it is God, the universe, nature, or whatever you believe in) does not like a vacuum, so it provides something to fill in the gap. I was truly touched by this law when I first heard it. It made more sense to me as I thought about how it actually works.

When it seems you have lost something, just remember it's all part of the perfect order because the Law of Vacuum will fill in the space created as a result of the 'loss'.

Be grateful for what seems like loss and anticipate something else to be aligned with your purpose and passion to fill the gap created by the loss. You see, the perfect order dictates that the Law of Vacuum will work to your advantage. All you have to do is look for it!

"Be fearless and pure; never waver in your determination...

Give freely. Be self-controlled, sincere, truthful, loving, and full of the desire to serve... Cultivate vigor, patience, will, purity; avoid malice and pride. Then, you will achieve your destiny."
Lord Krishna

To sum up this chapter, remember that the perfect order is here to serve everyone. Dr. John DeMartini's quote, "There are no mistakes in the universe," changed my life to such an extent that I have complete faith in the universe. Everything that is happening to us is a result of the perfect order working itself through our lives.

Start looking for the perfect order working in your life, and you will find signs of its existence.

You are part of the perfect order.

Self Assessment

If I did an honest evaluation of my life right now, would I see signs of the perfect order?

_____

_____

How will I realize the perfect order in my life?

_____

_____

What will it do for me when I realize the perfect order in my life?

_____

_____

Now, let's welcome you to the next chapter, **Higher Inspiration and Empowerment**.

Chapter 11

Welcome to Higher Inspiration and Empowerment

"Defeat is a state of mind. No one is ever defeated until defeat has been accepted as reality. To me, defeat in anything is merely temporary, and its punishment is but an urge for me to greater effort to achieve my goal. Defeat simply tells me that something is wrong in my doing; it is a path leading to success and truth."
Bruce Lee

When I finished high school, I did not get the score I aimed for to gain entry into my desired university course. At the time, I felt a sense of defeat. This was not a pleasant feeling. Back then, I did not know anything about personal development. I was barely an adult, still with a school boy image. Little did I realize that my low score was simply a revelation of the perfect order. It did not mean that I would never ever gain entry into my desired university course which was Bachelor of Business in Financial Planning. I clearly remember my dad telling me, "Don't worry. This could be a blessing in disguise. You'll be just fine." Yet my mental response was, "How could I be just fine??? I have worked so hard to get into that course, and now I won't. So, how could I just be fine?"

To me, this was a big problem. As I quoted Kerry Riley earlier on in the book, "Problems are gifts and blessings in disguise." Well, that is exactly what my dad, whom I consider to be a very wise man, was telling me at the time. I was just so consumed by defeat that my dad's words of wisdom did not enter my senses at all.

Time passed and I was accepted into another course, Bachelor of Commerce. My mind was still set on getting admission into the Bachelor of Business in Financial Planning. My game plan was to do my first year of tertiary education at the course I got accepted into, then transfer into the Bachelor of Business in Financial Planning. This meant I would need high scores in all my subjects to transfer into my desired course. I kept my eye on my goal and had full faith that I would achieve it.

During my first year, I was blessed to have met a fellow student, named Khunno, who, like me, wanted to transfer into another course. We became good friends and worked hard on our common goal. He kept me motivated and I did the same for him. We studied together for exams, did group assignments together and most importantly formed a solid bond. To this day, I consider Khunno one of my brothers, not friends. I gained a true friend for life, all thanks to my "blessing in disguise." Had I not taken this detour, I would not have met my treasured friend. Even though I did not want to be there in the first place, I met many great people and enjoyed my experience during my first year of tertiary education.

"Every dream that you have, was created by your powers to make these dreams come true. So why do you keep them inside you? Bring them out. Turn your dreams into your goals and achieve them!"
Ronny K. Prasad

Thankfully, my persistence, faith and work paid off and I got scores high enough to gain admission into the Bachelor of Business in Financial Planning as a second year student. The sense of accomplishment was unbelievable. I had done what I aimed for, for the past few years. When I told my dad that I had got entry into my dream course, he was very proud of me and told me to keep at it. I was very excited to get entry into this course. I was also sad to leave the university where I had spent my first year. This meant saying good-bye to good friends I had made and the academics who taught me. At the end of the day, I got what I desired and worked so hard for. My dear friend also got admission into the course he hoped for. It was a case of mission accomplished for both of us.

Looking back, I still hold onto the lessons that I was blessed to learn from this experience.

Don't blow things out of proportion or pretend it's the end of the world if I do not initially achieve what I was going for.

Every problem brings with it equal blessings. The times I enjoyed during my first year of tertiary education were the best days of

my university education. The friends for life I made here were priceless.

There is no such thing as defeat unless I choose to see it that way. Just because my high school score was a drawback, that did not mean I was defeated.

"Winners never quit and quitters never win."
Vince Lombardi

Always ask yourself for more. If you settle for less, you are allowing yourself to accept something which falls short of your desires. This, in my opinion, is not only a mistake, it's an attitude. Don't settle for less, no matter how challenging the situation may seem at the time. If you settle for less, you start breeding complacency! Beware of complacency, which robs you of making your dreams into reality.

There is a great man that I know, called Darren Burrows. Darren is a boxing trainer, who gives a priceless piece of advice to boxers who fight under his guidance. His exact words are:

"Never leave a decision in the hands of the judges!"

Darren's advice is related to boxing, meaning they should win a fight fair, without relying on a judge's decision if the match gets complicated.

The same can be applied to anyone's life, outside of the boxing ring. Sometimes people get too caught up in thinking about being 'judged' by others and leave their lives in the hands of other authority figures to determine what they should or should not do!

My suggestion is to be your own judge if you wish to live an authentic life according to your values. Then you will live by Darren's advice, and not leave things in the hands of other judges.

"True fulfillment is an awakening of consciousness. It comes from you, rather than to you."
Rhianna Fowler

I spoke about values in Chapter 2. If you live by your values, then why would you leave your results in the hands of other people, other judges? To be truly congruent to your values, start making your own decisions without fearing what other people might think. While making decisions, only take the counsel of people who understand you, and know what your values are. If they are in a position to offer their insights, you can integrate their insights into your decisions, at your discretion.

Please bear in mind that you allow other people's judgments to affect your actions or results. You can choose right now to separate judgement or counsel from people who don't know or understand your values.

One of my values is compassion. This compassion extends to humans and animals. I am kind and helpful toward people, without the intent of ever harming anyone, and I don't support anything which involves cruelty to animals.

There are times in my life, when I extend my compassion towards others, and people will advise me not to be so giving or caring. They generally back up their advice by telling me how they put boundaries in place regarding helping others. I agree that healthy boundaries are necessary. However, when I recognize that others are projecting their boundaries onto me, I remind myself that everyone's boundaries are different. If they do not see my boundaries as healthy, I know they do not understand my values. So, would I be wise to take their counsel? Of course not!

I believe in sharing my knowledge with others, and helping increase their awareness, without imposing my own values or ideals!

With all my clients, I get a clear understanding of their values, then I offer my support and insights. Most people who cast their judgements onto you have little or no understanding of your values. You will see this time and time again in your life.

"Set your sights high, the higher the better. Expect the most wonderful things to happen; not in the future but right now."
Eileen Caddy

When you are truly inspired, you have little time or energy to worry about possible judgements other people might cast upon you because you are too busy focusing on goals which support your purpose.

Purpose? Yes, purpose. My role is to support you to live your purpose with passion!

So, take a moment to address this question,

What is my purpose?

My purpose is to empower and inspire you, and to protect animals from cruelty. Do you have a purpose? I truly believe that each and every one of us has a purpose!

To help you in finding your purpose, please read the following, written by my dear friend and mentor Keith Leon:

Life Purpose

I spent many years searching for my answer to the questions: "Who am I?" and "What is my purpose?" During those years I did an extensive outer search. I visited every church I could find, looking for something or someone to show me the way to the answers I was seeking. I wished that I could sit down in front of people that I considered to be successful and ask them questions about life purpose and their discovery.

At one critical time during my inquiry I found myself a single father who had just ended a thirteen year marriage. I had no idea who I was. Because I had met my now ex-wife at such an early age, I only knew who I was with her. I found myself with a big empty hole and I had no idea how to fill it.

After wasting much time actively trying to figure it all out in my head, I decided that I needed to go within and listen for my answers. Fortunately, I had learned from a church how to quiet my mental noise, ask questions, and receive answers from my inner guidance. So, the pain I was feeling and the confidence I gained in listening to my inner voice motivated me to spend the next year meditating on the question, "Who Am I?"

From that came the questions: "What is my purpose?" and "Why am I here?" I would ask these questions one at a time, and I refused to do anything else (except to go to work, or to deal with immediate family issues) until I received my answers. I spent each waking moment waiting in the silence for answers to just "drop in." After many months of eager anticipation, the answers started to present themselves to me!

1. "Who am I?" I asked. I heard, "You are a child of infinite spirit. You are pure energy. You are actually living proof that God exists. You are a wonderful way that joy, love, happiness, melody, truth and compassion are happening on this planet you call home."

2. "What is my purpose?" I asked. I heard, "To teach and inspire the masses to know that they are perfect just the way they are. The gifts you have been given are innate; it is your purpose to share them. Keep them not inside of you, instead let these feelings, stories and sounds OUT, and those who are ready will hear what they need to hear and be moved by them."

3. "Why am I here?" I asked. I then heard, "You are here to touch the lives of each person you come in contact with. You are here to remember all that you have forgotten. You are here to love and be loved, and to learn to just be in each moment."

I asked my inner voice, "But how am I to teach and inspire the masses as a singer and songwriter?" "Yes," the voice said. "What about as an author, a teacher or as a preacher?" Again, I heard, "Yes." "Wait, which one?" I asked. All I heard was silence. "Which one?" I asked again and again. There was still no answer to my question.

I soon came to the realization that the answer to this question would be revealed either to me or through me at another other time. I had received the answers I needed to hear regarding my purpose already. This came with grace.

It wasn't until I started trying to figure out how that my clarity started to cloud up on me. I decided not to focus on the how, but to allow my inner knowing or instincts to point me in the right direction.

There is no one who can answer the question of your life's purpose better than your own inner guidance system. I've heard this inner guidance system called by many different names. I've heard it called God, instinct, the still small voice, Holy Ghost and many other names. You can call it what ever you like. I just know it's there for me when I am willing to sit and listen. Sometimes people ask me how is it that I hear voices in my head, and I say, "It's easier than you think."

Let me explain:

Start by sitting down. Turn off the noise of the world, and your random passing thoughts, and just listen. Listen to your breath at first, until you hear only your breath. If thoughts come in, let them pass through as quickly as they come and go back to your breath. Once all you hear is your breath, then work on turning off the sound of your breath, too. There is much revealed in the space between two breaths when you are tuned in and listening.

Sometimes this voice shows up as an inner knowing. You just all of a sudden become crystal clear on something you were wondering about before. You may hear a voice literally. I think the bottom line is to know and remember that you have every answer to every question within you. The question really is, are you willing to slow down enough to listen?

We as human beings seek incessantly, thinking there is so much we need to learn. Most of us have allowed ourselves to become human doings, not human beings! Plus, with all the external noise and activity in our lives, it's easy to forget how to use our innate ability to tune in to the guidance available through our thoughts and feelings.

Until we stop, slow down, turn off the television set, the stereo, the video games, or the opinions of our friends, co-workers or mates, we're unable to hear the wisdom that is within each of us.

Welcome To Your Life

It is ALL inside of you. I urge you to consider that perhaps we already know everything and just need to stop and listen, in order to remember. Everything you need to know is already within you. You are the answer you have been searching for!!!

Keith Leon is known as, "The Book Guy." With his wife Maura, Keith co-authored the book, *The Seven Steps to Successful Relationships*. With acclaimed authors, John Gray and Terry Cole Whittaker, Keith authored the best-selling book, *Who Do You Think You Are? Discover the Purpose of Your Life*, with a foreword by *Chicken Soup for the Soul's* Jack Canfield.

Keith was recently published in three new books: *The Power of Persistence* by Justin Sachs, *The Big Book of You* by Jennifer McLean, and *If I Can You Can* by Warren Henningsen. *If I Can You Can* was published by Keith's publishing company Babypie Publishing and reached Amazon International Best-Seller status the day it launched.

Keith's passion is teaching people how to go from first thought…to best seller! His passion is inspiring and teaching people to FINISH the book they've wanted to write for so long, and to help 1000 consultants, coaches, service professionals & entrepreneurs to do just that in 2011. Find out more at: www.TheyCallMeTheBookGuy.com

"Everything you need to know is already within you.
You are the answer you have been searching for."
Keith Leon

I believe that connecting with your purpose is the only way to live a life of empowerment, fulfillment, and inspiration.

When I discovered my purpose, I knew exactly what I needed to do, and what I wanted to do.

Once you discover your purpose, you will be inspired to take action. Please remember, if your purpose is self-centered without any contribution to the wider world, you will only grow to a certain extent. On the other hand, if your purpose is something that benefits you, and the wider world, you will experience more growth and personal fulfillment than you could possibly imagine!

> *"Adding value to other people's lives makes your life more valuable."*
> **Ronny K. Prasad**

When I made a firm commitment to myself to live my purpose, I knew I would get so much in return for what I was doing for the wider world. I am not saying the reason to live my purpose was for personal gain! You will be rewarded in some form or another once you start to live your purpose. My contribution made me smile from ear to ear.

Then I found passion in my purpose. Remember, I said that I am here to support you to live your purpose with passion? Well, that is exactly what I did! I believe in leading by example and I found a vehicle that supported my purpose and values, in a way nothing had before.

The passion that I am talking about is the 'Juice' that drives me to live my purpose. There are times when I am awake till the very early hours of the morning, writing an article on personal development, or responding to a client's email. Then I will wake up with a spring in my step, after having four or five hours of sleep because it is time to go for a run! The 'Juice' makes me wake up with a spring in my step! I love it, I absolutely love it.

I once read the definition of J.U.I.C.E – Join us in creating excitement!

If I am to give you a personal example, it would be this: who cares if I have only had four or five hours of sleep. I am 'juiced' up to go for a run, because I am grateful for the opportunity to run in the mornings! That is my definition of passion.

When I was executive coaching Dr. Graeme Smith, Order of Australia Medal holder, I was amazed at the passion he had about the work he was doing! I clearly remember one morning, he had to wake up at 4am to board an airplane for a business trip to Sydney, where he had a series of meetings lined up for the day, only to fly back to Melbourne later that night. I commented, "You have a long day ahead Graeme." He calmly replied, "That is alright, it will be a good long day!"

So, once you connect with your purpose, live your purpose with passion! That is when you get to realize that life is a wonderful journey!

> *"I am too inspired to be tired."*
> **Warren Henningsen**

When you have this 'juice' running through your veins, you will be too busy to be tired, or bored, or to pay attention to people casting judgements on you.

You will often get advice from people who know little about your values, and project their sense of righteousness onto you. Acknowledge them, and express your gratitude for giving their advice. Realize they are doing it out of good intent, and that they do not mean any harm to you. Having said that, ask yourself if their counsel is congruent to your values?

By now, I hope you have discovered your purpose. Once you have discovered your purpose, you can start setting goals which support it. If you need further clarity on discovering your purpose, please consider getting a coach or a mentor, who will assist you in finding your purpose in life.

Setting goals to support your purpose is like building a rocket ship which will launch you to the planet of your design! Goal-setting is a very important step in living your purpose. Setting and achieving goals can be fulfilling and fun!

One of the best books I have ever read on goal-setting is the best seller *Beyond Dreaming* by goal-setting expert Brian Leaning-Mizen.

Brian clearly defines the process of goal-setting in this book, and how setting goals will enable you to live your purpose.

My suggestion to you is to do write down your goals. That is the first step. Then break them down into finer details. For example, in my case one of my short-term goals was to get three new clients in a particular month, and donate 10% of my fees to them, to animal charities.

So when I wrote my goal down, it looked like this:

By this specific date, I will have a specific number of new clients whom I will inspire and empower, and 10% of my fees to them, would be donated to Animals Australia.

This goal was defined in terms of time, the number of clients, and what percentage of my fees would go to an exact animal charity, so the results were simple, measurable and I could track my progress.

> *"Give to the world the best you have,*
> *and the best will come back to you."*
> **Madeline Bridges**

Did you notice that this goal is aligned with my purpose?

When you set goals which are aligned with and support your purpose, you are simply unstoppable! It is a simple law of the universe!

So, right now, please pause for a moment, and write down a short term goal that aligns with and supports your purpose.

*By (dd/mm/yy)*_____,

I will _____,

*and*_____!

Now, your short term goal does not have to include donating money to a charity. It could be anything in terms of contributing towards a greater purpose. You could say that you will do some volunteer work.

For example, if your goal is to start playing the guitar, you could say something along the lines of: *By December 31st this year, I will have been taking guitar lessons, and I will play the guitar for my little nephew and niece, who appreciate music!*

Or, *By December 31st this year, I will have saved $5,000, which I will use to take my family on a holiday to our favourite destination.*

Play around with this concept, and set at least 2 short terms goals.

Once you have achieved these short term goals, write down a medium term, and a long term goal. The definition of medium term and long term comes purely at your discretion. You can decide what period of time constitutes medium term and long term goals.

What I am saying here is this, if you have a dream, turn it into a goal, and then turn it into an achievement. In other words;

$$\text{Dreams} \Rightarrow \text{Goals} \Rightarrow \text{Achievements}$$

Having clear and defined goals will give you:

The 4 C's (as mentioned in Chapter 4 in relation to affirmations):

- Confidence
- Clarity
- Certainty
- Capability

Which then leads to:

The 4 D's:

- Determination
- Desire
- Drive
- Devotion

> *"I believe that the three most powerful and important forces in the entire universe are in order: 1) Love 2) Respect 3) Honesty. Love can move mountains. It is the basis for the law of attraction. Respect is the thing we show others when we have it for ourselves. It is a by-product of love and can only be found in people that love themselves as well as everyone else, unconditionally. Honesty is the thing that ties it all together. We meet, we talk, I show you respect and you show me respect. It's all good."*
> **Dave Cobb**

Years ago, I was at a seminar where I heard Bob Proctor speak. During the break, I went up to Bob and asked him to sign an autograph for my friend Kimiko who had introduced me to the marvellous teachings of Bob Proctor. I loved the way Bob signed "Kimiko, keep your eye on your goal." That taught me a lot. The main thing that I learned was not to lower the standard of my goal!

I strongly suggest reading *Beyond Dreaming* by Brian Leaning-Mizen to learn the art of goal-setting. I have only given you slight insights into goal-setting. Brian goes into much deeper details about how to set, review, and achieve goals.

When I first contacted Brian, his message to me was, "Ron, make your name known to the world!" I was very inspired by his empowering advice to me!

> *"You dream, you believe, you create, you succeed."*
> **Trevor Hendy**

When it comes to setting goals, think big! In his book, *Think Big*, Dr. Ben Carson outlines the importance of thinking big, and he suggests applying 'thinking big' in every area of your life, not just in terms of goal-setting.

Practice thinking big, in all areas of your life. My belief on practice is this:

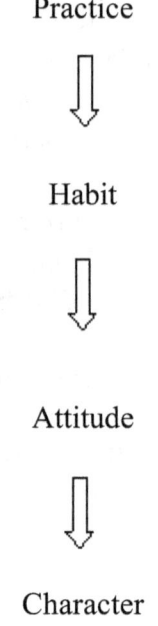

Practice

⇩

Habit

⇩

Attitude

⇩

Character

Make thinking big part of your character! It will serve you towards living your purpose with passion, supported by your goals. Just remember, if you think big, you are in a better position to act big. Which means your results will be big!

"That which does not kill us, only makes us stronger."
Friedrich Nietzsche

Very few people will ever achieve a major goal in life without setbacks. If you are someone who has done that, please consider yourself to be in the minority! Setbacks are an important part of the process of achieving your goals. Setbacks make you stronger and make the taste of victory even sweeter. Sometimes setbacks are needed for your growth. Setbacks have also the potential to act like a misleading image that you are not going to achieve your goals. When this happens, it pays to delete that misleading image and paint a picture of success.

Setbacks can push you back. Just how far back you are pushed entirely depends on you.

A classic example of this type of a scenario is the basketball great Michael Jordan. Did you know that he did not represent his high school on the basketball team in tenth grade? It was a setback and he saw through it. Then, he went on to become arguably the greatest basketball player that history has ever seen. He won five Most Valuable Player awards in the National Basketball Association. He has also been named the Athlete of the Century and has won the Sportsman of the Year award. The name Michael Jordan is immortal. His achievements speak for themselves.

"Obstacles don't have to stop you. If you run into a wall, don't turn around and give up. Figure out how to climb it, go through it, or work around it."
Michael Jordan

Keeping your eye on your goal (which supports your purpose), in the face of a setback, is like an insurance policy which ensures you will get over the hurdle that lies in front of you. I once heard "If life kicks you, let it kick you forward." Wow, what a brilliant piece of advice in regards to facing obstacles. You will have to absorb the impact of the kick, and it would be worth the pain the kick gives you. However, as a result of the pain, you would move forward.

Accept the pain and be consumed by it, or accept the movement forward and keep moving on. The choice is entirely yours.

Temporary setbacks are there to bring into order the Law of Equilibrium, which dictates that ultimately everything will equilibrate. To achieve your goals, the Law of Equilibrium will throw tests at you. You might have heard of 'What you give is what you get.' That is the Law of Equilibrium at work!

"Triumph often is nearest when defeat seems inescapable."
B.C. Forbes

Quoting Dr. Norman Vincent Peale, "Look down at your problems." The only way to look down on your obstacles is to rise above them. Dr. Norman Vincent Peale also stated that looking down on our problems gives us a more encouraging view. I totally agree with that statement. With encouragement, you will gain faith to get over this obstacle. What a beautiful analysis of faith and how we can use it to conquer life's obstacles. Faith keeps you looking up in life and not looking down.

Even if you face very big challenges, just remember the challenge will not be there forever if you focus enough on ways to get beyond it. Just like at sunset, the sun falls below the horizon and it becomes dark. It does not stay dark forever. In the morning the sun rises and darkness no longer prevails. Likewise in life, a temporary setback, it is not a permanent fall.

"If you have a dream, protect it
(from yourself and from others)."
Anonymous

This quote above perfectly sums up the importance of holding onto a dream. Once the dream is taken away from you, so will the desire to live that dream. Any chance you had to achieve your goal and live your dream will disappear.

So, protect your dream! I cannot be any more emphatic about this. Protect your dream. Your dream is the starting point which leads to your goal. Build an unbreakable desire to turn your dream into a goal, and then achieve that goal. Keep any undesired results out of your mind! I have seen many people (myself included) say things like, "But what if?"

When setting goals, focus on the actual goal and not on anything else. Some people like to have a contingency plan, or a Plan 'B'. That may be OK, as long as the focus is on the goal. Hence, the focus should be only on the goal. As Bob Proctor said to my dear friend Kimiko, "Keep your eye on your goal." I would have been stunned had Bob said, "Keep your eye on your contingency plan, just in case things go wrong!"

As you know, the Dark Room analogy indicates you will get what you focus on. Stay away from saying things like "I hope I do not fail, I hope things don't fall apart, I hope all my work is not wasted." These statements are not supporting your goals, which support your purpose.

> *"Life is a series of races. There are lessons in every race. There are life lessons to be learned every single day. If you don't win the race, but you get the lesson, and grow, you are truly a success. Live Your Dreams..."*
> **Jill Koenig**

Use persistence and perseverance to keep moving in the direction of your goals.

Persistence can be described as a fixed adherence to a resolve. By persisting, you keep doing whatever it takes to reach your goals. Give it your all. Persistence can and will make the difference when it comes to achieving your goals. Link the word persistence to the word stubborn when working towards a goal. Stubbornness can mean being very firm and not giving in. Likewise, persistence is all about not giving in. See yourself as being very stubborn in achieving your goals which support your purpose.

As Napoleon Hill said in *Think and Grow Rich*, "Those who have cultivated the habit of persistence seem to enjoy insurance against failure." You may now ask, "How do I build persistence?" Well, the answer lies in being determined enough to achieve your goal. The more determined you are, the more persistent you will be. Keep working on your goal and focus on the work you think is required to achieve that goal. Remind yourself that you are a step closer to achieving your goal. I would strongly suggest reading the chapter on Persistence in *Think and Grow Rich*.

Perseverance can be defined as continuing to strive in spite of difficulties. Make perseverance and persistence an important part of your life when you are working to achieve a goal. Mix these two together and you will gain an attitude which says "Persistence and Perseverance are here to serve me and support me, in achieving my goals, which support my purpose".

Life will present you with opportunities. Whether you choose to make the most out of these opportunities or not, is entirely up to you.

Use your awareness to recognize these opportunities, and grab them when you can. Once your awareness shifts, you will start seeing opportunity after opportunity. Things you would have normally not noticed will be right in front of you. Take advantage of the opportunities presented to you, whether they come slowly or quickly. In some cases, opportunity will not present itself for a long time. Being prompt is also important.

> *"Men who are resolved to find a way for themselves, will always find opportunities enough; and if they do not lie ready to their hand, they will make them."*
> **Samuel Smiles**

What is the point in looking back at missed opportunities in the past? Leave them there. Some people will live in the past, crying over missed opportunities. Please separate yourself from such people. Always be on the look-out for new opportunities. Life will present them to you. It is up to recognize these opportunities and then grab with both hands. Don't let go at any cost.

> *"The thing that really motivates me lies in the knowledge that I'm trying to make the most of who I am and what I have every day…and that's why it's so important for me to live life in a truly meaningful way."*
> **Cathy Freeman**

When I realized the accident I experienced as a child had impaired my vision and my eyes would never be the same as most other people's, I had to believe this was an opportunity to build on! I totally refused to compromise my life and kept moving forward. I refused to let this setback make me live my life any different to other people. I do not feel I am any different to any of my family, friends or associates because of my impairment. I know I am here to live life to the fullest and nothing can stop me if I do not allow myself to be stopped.

Sometimes life does not seem fair. Well, if you remember that the perfect order is making things happen, then life is fair!

Live life to the fullest, or as my dear friend, Josh Hinds, who is known as Mr. Motivation to others would say, "LIVE BIG." No one's life will be perfect in every single way. It's your job to look at imperfect things in a way that makes it look perfect.

Sometimes you will not utilize your potential until you are pushed beyond your reasonable limit. When I set out to pursue a career in personal development, my dear friend, Keith Ready told me that I needed to believe in myself. In other words, I do not need the support of someone else or any other outside influence. All I needed was to believe in myself. At the time, I was 29 years old I and I convinced myself that I had 29 years of lessons behind me and, that my faith would make me achieve any goal I wanted to achieve. I have been privileged enough to have Keith guide me in my journey and to this day, I am very thankful to have Keith as my friend and mentor.

It was a very important message to me, when Keith told me that I had to have my own backing. To me, self-motivation is a very powerful means to help me achieve my goals.

In his book *S.O.S (Secrets of Success)*, John Lane-Smith wrote, "Self-motivation is Life-force Energy." He referred to this as S.M.I.L.E.

John asked me to share with the readers of this book, the power of S.M.I.L.E. It amazes me that in the acronym above or in the original meaning, how a smile is such a powerful thing.

These are John's exact words:

"After the steering wheel collapsed my face during a car accident. I realized how much smiling is a gift, and it lead me to ask what happens inside. We know the effect on others or ourselves if others don't smile as you say. But what is happening inside? When my surgeon wired my jaw back on, he had to thread a wire up through my muscles, to lock it into my skull to hold my jaw in place for it to mend. If he had damaged either of those muscles I would not be able to smile now.

Because smiling was so important for me I started studying the effects in reverse. To smile feels good, it works, and makes us smarter in the process."

To find out more about John, please go to http://www.eclatpeoplesolutions.com.au/. John has just agreed to have his book published in French. (Reussir á tout prix!) So, the message of S.M.I.L.E will be reaching even more people!

I truly believe that self-motivation is unparalleled by any other form of motivation. Those of us who have been encouraged by self-motivation know too well what a wonderful gift it is to receive and apply.

Once you have achieved your goals, set new goals, look for new challenges, and start working on achieving them. I had not even finished writing this book and I was already in the process of coming up with a title for my next book. Setting new goals will keep you moving forward and take you above to higher places. It is very important to keep yourself growing, developing, and evolving. More challenges and goals will keep us stimulated mentally, emotionally, spiritually, and physically.

Please keep educating yourself. Education is never ending, it never stops. The more you learn, the more likely you are to achieve your goals.

I often tell people, "I am a permanent student at the Institute of Self Education."

This is attributed to my constant reading of books, listening to CDs, teleseminars, webinars, asking people for their insights, and learning from everything presented in front of me.

"The battle of life is, in most cases, fought up-hill; and to win it without a struggle was perhaps to win it without honour. If there were no difficulties, there would be no success; if there were nothing to struggle for, there would be nothing to be achieved. Difficulties may intimidate the weak, but they act only as a wholesome stimulus to men of resolution and valour."
Samuel Smiles

Imprint those words of a great man on your mind if you are to stand firm in the face of adversity and persevere.

Remember that challenges lead to success. It would not be ideal for you if your goals were served on a silver platter without your having to work for them or face challenges. If life was always smooth sailing, there would be no room for growth in any aspect of our existence. You would become stagnant and not move forward.

Develop a tremendous faith in yourself and let this faith be unbreakable. Let this faith remind you that you are capable of achieving your goals by standing tall in the face of adversity. Read out aloud the words of Samuel Smiles and tell yourself that if there were no challenges, there would be no success.

"Learn to enjoy every minute of your life. Be happy now. Don't wait for something outside of yourself to make you happy in the future. Think how really precious is the time you have to spend, whether it's at work or with your family. Every minute should be enjoyed and savoured."
Earl Nightingale

Also, pay particular attention to who you associate with the most. It is often said that you become whom you associate with. If people around you are bringing you down constantly, do not allow their negativity to consume you. Look for people who will make you grow and be part of your success. "He who walks with the wise grows wise, but a companion of fools suffers harm (Proverbs 13:20 NIV)." Just remember that Greatness gravitates to Greatness. Surround yourself with great people and great ideas. Then, watch the power of greatness unfold in beautiful ways.

Or, as Tony Robbins puts it, "You can walk in the shadows of minnows, or you can stand on the shoulders of giants."

In the book *Zen Flesh, Zen Bones* by Paul Reps, there is a reference to 'Taming the Bull'. The bull is referred to as your thoughts. When one thought arises, another thought follows. So if the first thought arises from enlightenment, all subsequent thoughts are enlightening! Likewise, when you have empowered and inspirational thoughts, more such thoughts will follow, putting you in a better position to achieve your goals.

Welcome To Your Life

The title of this book is *Welcome to Your Life*. I would suggest that you officially welcome yourself to your life right at this very moment. Make use of the methods of application in this book and live your purpose with passion! You have got the resources for winning the game of life, at your disposal right now. Use them. The sweetness of success is well worth the work that is required to get to your desired end result. Only you are capable of getting your success.

Go get it!

Don't Quit

When things go wrong, as they sometimes will.
When the road you are trudging seems all uphill
When funds are low and debts are high
And you want to smile but you have to sigh
When care is pressing you down a bit
Rest if you must, but don't you quit

Life is queer with its twists and turns
As every one of us sometimes learns
And many a failure turns about
When he might have won, he stuck it out
Don't give up though the pace seems slow
You may succeed with another blow

Often the goal is nearer than
It seems to faint and falter man
Often the struggler has given up
When he might have captured the victor's cup
And he leaned too late, when the night slipped down
How close he was to the golden crown

Success is failure turned inside out
The silver tint of the clouds of doubt
And you never can tell how close you are
It may be near when it seems afar
So stick to the fight when you are hardest hit
It's when things seem worst, that you must not quit

Anonymous

Welcome To Your Life

It is said that we can live 40 days without food, 8 days without water, 4 minutes without air and only a few seconds without hope…

In ending this book, I give you hope. Bob Proctor said, "If you have hope, you have options."

I sincerely hope that we meet one day. When we do meet, please share your inspired and empowered self with me.

Thank you for allowing me to serve you in finding inspiration and empowerment.

Welcome to Your Life,

Ronny K. Prasad
www.ronnykprasad.com
ronnykprasad@yahoo.com.au

If you would like to subscribe to my newsletter Ideal Insights, please visit www.impetussuccess.com.au and enter your name and email address. I send these newsletters on a monthly basis.

I hope that you will enjoy reading my newsletters, and find them to be insightful to create lasting positive changes in your life.

Recommended Resources

Warren Henningsen – If I Can You Can book.
Warren is my personal mentor, and I am a graduate of his powerful Finding Zero mentorship program. Being an International Best Selling Author, Speaker, and Mentor, Warren has the ability to transform anyone's life with his wealth of knowledge and eagerness to create lasting empowering changes in people's lives. Please visit his website to purchase his book, and to learn more about the great man.
www.warrenhenningsen.com

Keith Leon – Who Do You Think You Are? book.
Keith is a dear friend, and a mentor who made this book possible! His knowledge about human behaviour, universal laws, personal relationships, and publishing books (of course) are worth learning from. He is a best-selling author, a relationships expert (along with his dear wife Maura), and an in-demand speaker. He has also co-authored 7 Steps to a Successful Relationship with Maura. His dedication to supporting people in achieving their goals is to be admired, indeed!
www.relationship-masters.com

Keith Ready – A Gift of Inspiration website
Keith Ready lives and works in Sydney, Australia and is affectionately known as Mr. Inspiration. He is the publisher of InspirEmail which provides fortnightly inspirational messages to refresh the spirit and boost the emotional bank account. I have had the honour of knowing Keith for well over 3 years. In that time, he has inspired me and guided me with his insights. Keith's website is now one of the world's most popular internet resources for positive inspirational stories, messages, quotes, and images. You can visit his website at . . .
www.agiftofinspiration.com.au or email him at
info@agiftofinspiration.com.au

Phil Evans – PeoplEmail
'Lucky' Phil is a coaching and mentoring guru. I have had the privilege of knowing 'Lucky' Phil for several years now. He is an amazing man,

with his insights on positive change, and willingness to create better lives for people all around the world!

I strongly recommend his Inspirational emails, PeoplEmail, which has been featured on Bob Proctor's Friday Story on a number of occasions. www.peoplestuff.com.au

Ari Galper – Unlock the Game

Ari is the founder of Unlock the Game, which takes the sales mindset to a new dimension. I am a member of Unlock the Game, and the effect it had on my professional and personal life, is beyond words. People all over the world are benefiting from Ari's training. Not to mention, that Ari is a very friendly and humble person!

I strongly recommend Unlock The Game to anyone in the sales industry. Please visit www.UnlockTheGame.com

Brian Leaning-Mizen – Beyond Dreaming book.

Brian is the founder and Principal of Mind Synergy, with over thirty years experience helping and encouraging people to achieve their dreams and goals. Brian is often referred to as The Guru of Goal Setting. His book Beyond Dreaming is an easy introduction to goal setting and remains a best seller.

Please visit www.mindsynergy.net

Dan Caro – The Gift of Fire: How I Made Adversity Work For Me book.

At the age of two, Dan sustained third degree burns to over seventy percent of his body. Ultimately, as a result of the burn injuries, Dan lost his right hand, most of his left hand and is severely scarred. In the mid-1980s, reconstructive surgery that would give Dan the use of a moveable thumb was performed on his left hand. Since then, Dan has been living life to the fullest in the face of his adversity. His relentless attitude and resiliency would consistently prove that nothing is impossible; including his lifelong dream of becoming a musician. In addition to music, Dan is an Ambassador for the Shriners of North America. He is a professional speaker who shares stories of fulfillment and achievement; A prime example of bravery and courage.

Please visit www.dancaro.com

Josh Hinds – www.getmotivation.com
Josh is an Entrepreneurial Educator and Motivational Speaker.
I first came into contact with Josh, when I went to his website, and signed up for his newsletter Motivation in a Minute, which is available at his website.
I love the way Josh encourages people to 'Live Big!'

David Boufford
David is affectionately known as Mr. Positive, with his powerful insights on maintaining a positive mindset! Dave's insights have helped me maintain a positive outlook in life!
He is referred to as the 'Professional Encourager,' because he has a passion for encouraging people! You can sign up for his emails on www.mrpositive.com

David Morelli
David is an expert when it comes to energy channelling meditations. He is also a transformational healer! His meditation teachings are among the best in the world. You can benefit more from David's teachings by going to his website www.enwaken.com

Graeme Alford – Never Give Up! book.
Graeme is one of Australia's leading motivational speakers and writers. His book Never Give Up! was a best seller.
You can learn more about Graeme by visiting his website www.motivationalfocus.com

John Lane-Smith – Secrets of Success book
John's book, Secrets of Success, is a very powerful guide on having the right attitude when it comes to attracting more success in your life. After a serious car accident, John wrote this book to share his insights into what success means, and how to have more of it into your life.
You can find out more about John by visiting
 www.eclatpeoplesolutions.com.au

Bibliography

If I Can You Can, Warren Henningsen, Babypie Publishing 2008

Who do you think you are? Keith Leon, Babypie Publishing, 2007

You were born Rich – Bob Proctor, LifeSuccess Publications, 1997

Self Help – Samuel Smiles, Oxford, 1859

The Winning Attitude – John C. Maxwell, Thomas Nelson Inc, 1993

The Psychology of Winning – Dr. Dennis Waitley, Berkeley Books, 1979

Think and Grow Rich – Napoleon Hill, Tarcher/ Penguin 2005

The Power of Positive Thinking – Dr. Norman Vincent Peale, Simon & Schuster, 1992

Deeper Insights – Kerry Riley, Future Energy Dimensions, 1987

Breaking Through Limitations – John Kanary, LifeSuccess Publications, 2003

The New Merriam-Webster Dictionary, Merriam Webster, 1989

The 7 Habits of Highly Effective People – Stephen R. Covey, Free Press, 1989

Zen Flesh, Zen Bones, Paul Reps, Pelican Books, 1971

Secrets of Success, John Lane-Smith, Angus & Robertson, 1992

The Science of Success, Wallace D. Wattles, Sterling Publishing Company, 2007

Think Big, Ben Carson, Zondervan, 1992

Beyond Dreaming, Brian Leaning-Mizen, Wrightbooks, 1999

Never Give Up, Graeme Alford, McPherson's Printing Group, 1998

Synchro Destiny, Deepak Chopra, Rider, 2003

www.ingramcontent.com/pod-product-compliance
Lightning Source LLC
Chambersburg PA
CBHW071607170426
43196CB00033B/2134